ALEX BRIGHTWELL

Kickstart Your Day

Unleash Your Full Potential with Powerful Morning Routines Before 7AM

Copyright © 2024 by Alex Brightwell

All rights reserved. No part of this publication may be reproduced, stored or transmitted in any form or by any means, electronic, mechanical, photocopying, recording, scanning, or otherwise without written permission from the publisher. It is illegal to copy this book, post it to a website, or distribute it by any other means without permission.

Second edition

This book was professionally typeset on Reedsy.
Find out more at reedsy.com

Contents

Introduction	1
Chapter 1: The Science Behind Morning Routines	4
Understanding Circadian Rhythms	4
The Impact on Productivity	7
Chapter 2: The Benefits of Waking Up Early	11
Increased Morning Productivity	11
Mental Clarity and Focus	14
Chapter 3: Designing Your Perfect Morning	17
Identifying Your Goals	17
Creating a Custom Routine	20
Chapter 4: The Power of Consistency	23
Building Habits	23
Overcoming Obstacles	25
Chapter 5: Nutrition and Hydration	29
The Best Breakfasts for Energy	29
Hydration Tips	32
Chapter 6: Exercise and Movement	35
Morning Workouts	35
Stretching and Yoga Practices	38
Chapter 7: Mental and Emotional Wellbeing	41
Meditation Practices	41
Journaling for Clarity	44
Chapter 8: Planning and Setting Intentions	48
Daily Planning Techniques	48
The Role of Affirmations	51
Chapter 9: Personal Development	55

- Learning and Skill Building — 55
- Reading and Audiobooks — 58

Chapter 10: The Role of Sleep — 62
- Importance of Quality Sleep — 62
- Sleep Hygiene Tips — 66

Chapter 11: Case Studies and Success Stories — 69
- Famous Figures and Their Routines — 69
- Real-Life Testimonials — 73

Chapter 12: Tracking Your Progress — 76
- Keeping a Morning Routine Journal — 76
- Measuring Impact on Productivity — 79

Chapter 13: Adapting to Change — 82
- Adjusting Your Routine for Different Seasons — 82
- Coping with Unexpected Changes — 85

Chapter 14: Technology and Minimalism — 88
- Digital Detox Strategies — 88
- Essential Morning Apps — 91

Chapter 15: Creating a Morning Playlist — 95
- The Benefits of Music — 95
- Recommended Playlists — 99

Chapter 16: Family and Social Considerations — 102
- Involving Family Members — 102
- Balancing Social Commitments — 105

Chapter 17: Weekend Routines — 108
- Tailoring Your Weekend Mornings — 108
- Rest and Recreation — 111

Chapter 18: Morning Routines for Different Personalities — 114
- Tailoring Routines for Introverts — 114
- Tailoring Routines for Extroverts — 117

Chapter 19: The Role of Environment — 120
- Creating a Peaceful Space — 120
- Organizing Your Morning Environment — 123

Chapter 20: Overcoming Common Challenges — 126

Dealing with Procrastination	126
Battling Morning Fatigue	129
Chapter 21: The Importance of Reflection	132
End-of-Month Reviews	132
Adjusting for Continuous Improvement	135
Chapter 22: The Long-Term Impact of Morning Routines	139
Studies on Longevity and Health	139
Career and Personal Growth	142
Chapter 23: Creating a Morning Routine Community	145
Finding Accountability Partners	145
Joining Online Groups and Forums	148
Chapter 24: Custom Routines for Specific Goals	151
Routines for Entrepreneurs	151
Routines for Students	154
Chapter 25: Reinforcing Your Routine with Evening Habits	158
Preparing the Night Before	158
Unwinding Techniques	161
Conclusion	165
Appendix A: Appendix	168
Sample Morning Routines	168
Additional Resources and Suggested Readings	171

Introduction

Imagine waking up each morning with a sense of purpose, enthusiasm, and clarity. Picture starting your day feeling energized and ready to tackle whatever challenges come your way. For many, this sounds like an unattainable dream. However, this ideal morning is closer than you think. It's not reserved for the lucky few. It's available to anyone willing to invest in themselves and take proactive steps toward creating a morning routine that sets the foundation for a productive and fulfilling day.

This book is designed to be your guide on a journey towards mastering your mornings. We'll dive deep into the essential elements of morning routines, uncover the science behind them, and show you how to tailor a regimen that aligns with your unique goals and lifestyle. By the time you've turned the last page, you'll possess the tools and knowledge to construct a morning ritual that empowers you to reach new heights in both your professional and personal life.

Why focus on mornings? Mornings are transformative. The first few hours after waking up set the tone for the rest of the day. They hold the power to either boost your productivity and wellbeing or leave you feeling stressed and unprepared. For ambitious professionals and individuals striving for personal growth, a well-crafted morning routine is a game-changer.

It all starts with understanding who you are and what you want. Are you looking to increase your productivity at work? Improve your mental clarity? Gain a sense of peace and balance before the demands of the day begin? Identifying your goals is the first step in designing a morning routine that works for you.

For productivity enthusiasts, the science behind morning routines and circadian rhythms will provide fascinating insights into how our bodies and minds work. You'll learn about the biological clock that influences your energy levels and moods, and how you can harness this knowledge to maximize your efficiency during those peak morning hours. From increasing your output to achieving a heightened state of focus, the evidence is compelling and actionable.

One key takeaway is the power of consistency. The most effective routines are those that become ingrained habits. It's not just about a one-time overhaul of your schedule; it's about creating sustainable practices that integrate seamlessly into your daily life. Persistence pays off, and we'll explore strategies to help you build and maintain these habits, even when faced with obstacles.

Nutrition, hydration, exercise, and mental wellbeing are foundational pillars of an exceptional morning. The food you consume, the fluids you drink, and the physical activity you engage in all play crucial roles in determining how your day unfolds. We'll provide you with practical advice and tips for fueling your body with the right nutrients and staying hydrated. We'll also delve into various forms of exercise, from intense morning workouts to calming yoga practices, helping you find what works best for you.

Your mental and emotional health is equally important. Incorporating practices like meditation and journaling into your mornings can cultivate a sense of inner peace and clarity. These activities are not just spiritual or therapeutic; they are powerful tools to sharpen your focus and enhance your emotional intelligence, preparing you to face any challenges that may arise.

Planning and setting intentions for the day ahead can significantly influence your ability to stay organized and motivated. Techniques for effective daily planning and the role of affirmations will be discussed, offering you methods to structure your to-do list in a way that aligns with your broader objectives.

All of these elements contribute to personal development and continuous growth. Whether it's through learning, skill-building, reading, or audiobooks, your mornings offer a prime opportunity for self-improvement.

Sleep can't be overlooked. Quality rest is essential to any successful

INTRODUCTION

morning routine, and we'll address both the importance of sleep and tips for maintaining good sleep hygiene, ensuring you wake up refreshed and ready.

You'll also be inspired by real-life case studies and success stories. Seeing how others have transformed their lives through morning routines can be incredibly motivating and offer valuable lessons.

We've ensured that this book is packed with practical advice and actionable steps, but it's also grounded in real-world experiences and scientific research. The aim is to provide a balanced approach that combines inspiration with concrete strategies that you can implement immediately.

Sure, there will be challenges along the way. Procrastination, morning fatigue, and the inevitable disturbances to your routine are all part of the journey. But armed with the insights and strategies from this book, you'll be well-equipped to face these hurdles head-on and emerge stronger.

Consider this book your roadmap to creating the best version of yourself, starting with how you begin your day. By dedicating time to thoughtfully design and refine your morning routine, you're investing in a foundation that will support every aspect of your life.

So let's embark on this journey together. The chapters that follow will provide you with a comprehensive blueprint for crafting a morning routine that is not only effective but transformative. Get ready to wake up to your full potential every single day. Your next level of productivity and personal growth starts here, in the quiet, powerful hours of the morning.

Chapter 1: The Science Behind Morning Routines

Unlocking the potential of your mornings begins with understanding the science behind how our bodies and minds are wired. At the core of this lies our circadian rhythms — natural, internal processes that regulate the sleep-wake cycle. By aligning your morning routine with these rhythms, you optimize your energy levels and mental acuity when they're at their peak. Research shows that a well-crafted morning routine not only boosts productivity but also sets a positive tone for the entire day. It's all about leveraging the first few hours after you wake up to maximize focus, creativity, and efficiency. When you harness the power of a structured morning routine, you tap into a heightened state of readiness and resilience, paving the way for greater personal and professional achievements.

Understanding Circadian Rhythms

To truly harness the power of an effective morning routine, it's essential to understand the underlying science of circadian rhythms. These natural cycles govern various physiological processes in our bodies, influencing when we feel awake and alert vs. when we crave rest. So, what exactly are circadian rhythms?

Circadian rhythms are 24-hour cycles that play a crucial role in our biological processes. These rhythms are predominantly controlled by an internal "biological clock" located in a part of the brain called the suprachiasmatic nucleus (SCN). Located in the hypothalamus, the SCN receives direct input from our eyes—which means light plays a significant role in regulating these rhythms.

When you wake up to natural light or a well-timed alarm in the morning, you're actually responding to your body's circadian signals. These signals help to reset the circadian clock, syncing it with the external environment. Conversely, when you're exposed to artificial light late at night, it can disrupt the natural progression of these rhythms, leading to poor sleep and reduced next-day performance.

In practical terms, understanding your circadian rhythms can be a game-changer for productivity. Imagine knowing the exact times during the day when you're at your peak performance. That's what understanding your body clock offers—an internal schedule tailored to maximize your alertness and efficiency.

Most people experience a natural dip in energy post-lunch, often referred to as the "afternoon slump." This is not simply due to the meal you've eaten but is a built-in aspect of your circadian rhythm. Recognizing this can prevent you from making unrealistic demands on yourself during these low-energy periods and instead schedule less demanding tasks for these times.

Your morning routine can be optimized by aligning activities with your circadian peaks. For instance, cognitive tasks or activities that require a lot of mental effort are usually best performed in the morning when your mind is sharpest. Physical activities like workouts can also be strategically scheduled based on when you are naturally most energetic, depending on whether you're a morning or evening person.

It's fascinating to note that not everyone has the same circadian rhythm. Some are "early birds," while others are "night owls." Early birds often find their peak alertness soon after waking up and benefit from starting their days early with complex tasks. Night owls, on the other hand, may find that their cognitive peak comes later in the day. The beauty of understanding your circadian rhythm lies in its ability to help you tailor your morning routine uniquely to fit your natural cycles.

Moreover, the regulation of important hormones like cortisol and melatonin are under the control of circadian rhythms. Cortisol, often referred to as the stress hormone, has its natural peak in the early morning, making it the perfect time to engage in activities that require a lot of mental focus and physical energy. Melatonin, the sleep hormone, is naturally higher in the evening, preparing your body for rest.

Incorporating mindfulness or meditation sessions in the morning could also be beneficial. Many individuals report heightened mental clarity and emotional stability from even short periods of morning meditation, effectively setting a calm and productive tone for the rest of the day. Understanding the natural ebb and flow of cortisol can help you decide the best times for these practices.

The impact of circadian rhythms extends beyond just sleep and wake cycles, though. They also influence digestion, body temperature, and various other bodily functions. When everything is in sync, you feel more balanced and attuned to your daily demands. However, disruptions to this balance can result in feelings of jet lag, even without traveling.

One of the most common disruptions to circadian rhythm is what researchers call "social jetlag." This often happens when there's a significant difference between your weekday and weekend sleep patterns. Sticking to a consistent wake-up time, even on weekends, can greatly enhance your body's ability to maintain a regular circadian rhythm, ultimately improving both sleep quality and daytime function.

Think of maintaining your circadian rhythm as a cornerstone of your overall health. When you're in sync, your body functions more efficiently, you sleep better, and you're more alert and productive during your waking hours. Therefore, the first step to designing an effective morning routine should always be assessing and understanding your natural circadian tendencies. By noting when you feel most awake and when you naturally start to wind down, you can begin to tailor your activities around these times.

There's a growing body of research showcasing the importance of timing, often referred to as "chronobiology." For ambitious professionals aiming to optimize their morning routines for peak productivity, aligning your schedule with your circadian rhythms can offer a tremendous advantage. Being aware of your body's natural rhythms helps you make informed decisions about when to tackle your most demanding tasks, when to rest, and even when to eat for optimal energy levels.

Finally, one of the most practical ways to align your morning routine with your circadian rhythm is through the use of light. Morning exposure to natural light triggers your body's internal clock to start the day, increasing alertness and mood. Simple practices like opening your curtains as soon as you wake up or taking a brief walk outside can immensely influence your body's rhythm.

In summary, understanding circadian rhythms is not just a scientific curiosity; it's a pragmatic approach to enhancing your daily routine. By tapping into the biological clock, you can design a morning routine that not only maximizes your productivity but also promotes overall wellbeing. Therefore, take the time to observe and understand your natural rhythms — it's the foundation upon which an effective, personalized morning routine can be built.

The Impact on Productivity

The impact of a well-structured morning routine on productivity cannot be overstated. When we start our day with intention and clarity, we set ourselves up for success. Let's delve deeper into the mechanisms of how a morning routine can turbocharge our productivity throughout the day.

Each morning brings a fresh slate, a new beginning that offers us the chance to shape our day the way we want. By establishing a personalized morning routine, we essentially front-load our day with positive actions that build momentum. This momentum acts as a catalyst, enabling us to tackle tasks more efficiently and with greater focus. Imagine starting your day with fifteen minutes of exercise: your body wakes up, endorphins are released, and you feel a sense of accomplishment that propels you into your workday with vigor.

Furthermore, morning routines provide a crucial period of uninterrupted time. In today's hyper-connected world, distractions are a common bane. Morning routines allow us to engage in activities free from interruptions, whether that's sipping a cup of coffee while planning the day or engaging in a focused work session. This period of solitude can lead to an enhanced state of flow, where we can accomplish more in less time.

Productivity isn't just about getting tasks done; it's about getting the right tasks done effectively. Morning routines that incorporate goal setting and prioritization make a huge difference. When we take a few moments to identify our key objectives for the day, we become more aligned with our bigger goals. This alignment ensures that our efforts are spent on high-impact activities, rather than getting bogged down by low-priority tasks.

Time management expert Laura Vanderkam often highlights how successful people leverage their mornings. They tend to focus on important work first, rather than getting caught up in reactive tasks like answering emails. This proactive approach to the day ensures that the most critical work gets done when our mental energy is at its peak.

Moreover, morning routines can foster a sense of control and empowerment. When you take charge of your morning, you set a precedent for the rest of the day. This sense of control can reduce anxiety and stress, which are often productivity killers. The American Psychological Association notes that managing stress effectively leads to better performance and productivity.

Psychologically, humans are creatures of habit. Establishing a consistent morning routine trains our brains to expect and prepare for specific activities. This consistency reduces decision fatigue, a phenomenon where the quality of decisions deteriorates after a long session of decision making. By automating the start of our day, we conserve mental energy for more complex tasks ahead.

Interestingly, the benefits of morning routines extend beyond individual productivity to organizational effectiveness. Companies with employees who maintain healthy morning routines report higher overall performance. When employees start their day with clarity and vigor, they bring that positive energy into the workplace, resulting in a more productive and harmonious environment.

It's important to recognize that a "one size fits all" approach doesn't work when it comes to morning routines. Tailoring your routine to fit your unique lifestyle and goals is crucial. Whether you're an entrepreneur who needs early morning quiet to brainstorm new ideas or a professional preparing for back-to-back meetings, your morning routine should cater to your individual needs.

Implementing a morning routine doesn't mean you have to overhaul your entire life. Small, incremental changes can lead to significant improvements over time. Start with simple adjustments, like drinking a glass of water immediately after waking up or spending five minutes journaling your thoughts. These small victories accumulate, creating a robust framework for sustained productivity.

Morning routines also contribute to mental clarity. Engaging in activities like meditation, deep breathing, or even light stretching can help clear the mental cobwebs that form overnight. This mental clarity allows for more precise and strategic thinking, which is invaluable in any professional setting.

Additionally, the act of completing a morning routine provides a sense of accomplishment. This creates a positive feedback loop, where the satisfaction of having completed meaningful activities fuels further productivity. When you start your day with a win, you're more likely to continue winning as the day progresses.

Of course, the benefits of a morning routine extend to time management. By following a set routine, you create time frames for various activities, thereby reducing procrastination. When you know you have a designated time to exercise, plan your day, and address immediate tasks, you're less likely to waste time figuring out what to do next.

An often-overlooked aspect of morning routines is the impact on creativity. Mornings are a prime time for creative work, as the brain is fresh and unburdened by the demands of the day. Engaging in creative pursuits early in the day can lead to breakthroughs and innovative solutions.

The morning also offers a unique opportunity for self-reflection. Moments spent in silence, prayer, or meditation can offer insights that might not surface during the busier parts of the day. This introspection can lead to a deeper understanding of one's goals and values, further enhancing the day's productivity.

Another powerful element involves visualization and affirmations. Taking a few minutes each morning to visualize your success and remind yourself of your goals can set a positive tone for the day. This practice aligns your mental state with your aspirations, making it easier to take the necessary steps to achieve them.

Science supports the link between morning routines and productivity. Studies on circadian rhythms show that our cognitive functions are often at their peak in the hours following awakening. Leveraging this natural boost can lead to enhanced problem-solving abilities and improved decision-making.

A crucial component often integrated into morning routines is physical activity. Whether it's a full workout, a quick jog, or gentle stretching, moving your body increases blood flow to the brain, thereby enhancing cognitive functions. Physical activity also promotes the release of neurotransmitters like dopamine and serotonin, which are vital for maintaining focus and motivation.

Morning routines also create a buffer zone before the demands of the day take over. This buffer allows you to prepare mentally and emotionally for the challenges ahead, leading to better coping mechanisms and resilience. When you start strong, you're better equipped to handle stressors and setbacks.

To summarize, the impact of a well-crafted morning routine on productivity is multi-faceted. It enhances focus, fosters creativity, reduces stress, and aligns daily activities with long-term goals. By setting the stage for a productive day, morning routines empower us to achieve more with greater efficiency and purpose. The true power lies not just in the activities themselves, but in the consistency and intention behind them. So, start small, stay committed, and watch as your productivity soars.

Chapter 2: The Benefits of Waking Up Early

Waking up early is more than just an admirable habit; it's a transformative way to enhance your life. Imagine the tranquility of the early morning hours: it's a unique, undisturbed period where your mind is clear and your energy unbridled. This uninterrupted time can become your secret weapon for increased productivity and mental clarity, allowing you to tackle high-priority tasks before the demands of the day take over. By aligning your waking hours with the natural rhythms of your body, you'll find it easier to focus, think creatively, and make better decisions. The quiet solitude of the morning offers a rare chance to center yourself, setting a positive tone that reverberates throughout the day. Whether it's through meditation, exercise, or planning your day, these early hours provide the perfect canvas to paint the day you want to live. Embrace the dawn, and unlock a myriad of benefits that can lead to staggering personal and professional growth.

Increased Morning Productivity

Imagine waking up early enough to experience tranquility, a world still asleep, as the dawn breaks. It's in these early hours that you can tap into a wellspring of productivity you might not have realized existed. Leveraging this time effectively can be a game-changer. Starting your day with tasks that require focus and creativity—whether it's strategic planning, deep work, or a personal project—is far easier when distractions are minimal, and your mind is at its freshest.

The magic of the early hours lies in their solitude. With fewer emails pinging your inbox, minimal interruptions from coworkers, and a quieter environment overall, you can get into a state of deep work far more efficiently. It's when the world is quieter that you can genuinely hear your own thoughts. This clarity allows for better problem-solving and creative thinking, setting the tone for a productive day ahead.

Not only do early mornings provide an ideal setting for deep work, but they also give you a psychological edge. Accomplishing significant tasks early on boosts your sense of achievement, creating a positive feedback loop that propels you throughout the rest of the day. Essentially, you're front-loading your day with productivity, which reduces stress and makes you feel more in control of your time.

One of the key aspects of increased morning productivity is the ability to focus on high-priority tasks without the pressure of immediate deadlines. Early hours can be purposefully reserved for strategizing, planning, or working on long-term projects. Without the constraints of immediate, reactive work, your mind can explore creative solutions and innovative ideas.

Morning productivity also thrives on routine. Establishing a consistent morning routine primes your brain for work. For many, this could involve a series of actions—waking up, exercising, meditating, and then diving into work. By committing to a repetitive sequence, you reduce decision fatigue and harness the power of habit, thereby increasing your efficiency.

The early hours also offer a sanctuary for personal growth activities. Reading, learning a new skill, or engaging in reflective practices like journaling are incredibly fruitful when your mind is unburdened by the day's demands. For ambitious professionals, integrating personal growth into morning routines ensures that self-improvement doesn't get sidelined by the busyness of the day.

Another benefit synonymous with early mornings is the chance to exercise undisturbed. Physical activity not only boosts your physical health but also revitalizes your mental state. A morning workout can enhance mood by releasing endorphins, reduce anxiety, and improve overall cognitive function. This physical uplift can provide a significant boost to your productivity

CHAPTER 2: THE BENEFITS OF WAKING UP EARLY

throughout the day.

When you wake up early, you've effectively stretched your day. While it's true that everyone gets the same 24 hours, the early riser often perceives having more time because their day starts with purpose and intention. By the time midday hits, they may have already accomplished what would take others a full day to achieve, freeing up their schedule to either take on more or to decompress.

The act of waking up early can also foster a mindset of discipline and control. When you choose to start your day on your terms, you assert control over your schedule rather than being at the mercy of it. This proactive stance can cascade into other areas of your life, making you more disciplined and intentional in your daily activities.

However, it's essential to note that simply waking up early is not a cure-all for productivity. The key lies in how you use this time. Structuring your morning with clear intentions, setting specific goals, and eliminating potential distractions are crucial steps. Invest your early hours in high-value activities that offer the most significant return on energy and effort.

In our hyper-connected world, digital distractions are ever-present. Morning productivity can be significantly enhanced by implementing a brief period of digital detox right after waking up. Instead of reaching for your phone to check emails or social media, use this time to engage in meaningful activities that set a positive tone for the day.

Lastly, sharing your morning productivity with others can amplify the benefits. Accountability partners or morning clubs can provide the motivation and camaraderie needed to sustain early rising habits. Engaging in this practice within a community can offer fresh perspectives, new strategies, and mutual support.

In summary, early mornings are ripe with potential. They offer uninterrupted time, a fresh start for creativity and focus, and an opportunity to engage in personal growth and physical activity. By crafting a purposeful morning routine aligned with your goals and sticking to it, you can harness the power of the early hours to boost your productivity and set yourself up for success. The benefits are not just professional but permeate every aspect of your life, paving the way for holistic growth and enhanced well-being.

Mental Clarity and Focus

Waking up early can do wonders for mental clarity and focus, offering you a head start in a world that's often consumed by noise and distractions. Early mornings, with their serene and quiet atmosphere, provide a golden opportunity to clear your mind and concentrate on what's truly important. This section delves into why and how waking up early can heighten your mental clarity and focus, setting you up for a successful and productive day.

Firstly, let's address the stillness of early mornings. When you wake up before the rest of the world, you're afforded a unique opportunity to engage in activities without interruptions. No urgent emails, no sudden calls, no mundane tasks pulling you in every direction. This uninterrupted time is a haven for your mind, allowing you to channel your energy into tasks that require undivided attention. Whether you're tackling a complex project, planning your day, or engaging in creative pursuits, the quiet hours of the morning can be especially conducive to deep, focused work.

Moreover, waking up early gives you the chance to engage in practices that boost mental clarity right from the start. For instance, meditation and mindfulness exercises are particularly effective in the early hours. When practiced regularly, these activities help to clear mental clutter, reduce stress, and improve concentration. Starting your day with a focused mind can act like a shield, protecting you from the chaos and distractions that may come later.

Nutrition also plays a key role in mental clarity and focus. By waking up early, you have the time to prepare a nutritious breakfast, rather than grabbing a quick, unhealthy snack on your way out the door. Foods rich in antioxidants, good fats, vitamins, and minerals provide the brain with the fuel it needs to function optimally. A healthy breakfast can improve cognitive function, boost memory, and keep you alert and focused throughout the day.

The connection between physical activity and mental clarity is another compelling reason to wake up early. Early risers often take advantage of the morning for exercise, which has been shown to release endorphins, reduce stress, and improve mood. These benefits extend to your mental state, enhancing your ability to concentrate. Even a simple morning walk can have significant positive effects on your cognitive functions.

Structured planning is another benefit of early mornings that shouldn't be overlooked. When you rise early, you grant yourself the time to plan and set intentions for the day. This proactive approach allows you to outline your goals, prioritize tasks, and mentally prepare for what lies ahead. A well-ordered day reduces anxiety and decision fatigue, freeing up mental resources to focus on meaningful work.

Early mornings also provide the ideal setting for a harmonious start to the day, which is critical for maintaining mental clarity. Waking up early affords you the luxury of immersing yourself in moments of inspiration, whether through reading, writing, or reflecting. These quiet moments of personal enrichment can make a marked difference in your overall mental state, fostering a sense of clarity and purpose that carries into the rest of your day.

Moreover, waking up early helps maintain a consistent sleep schedule, aligning your body's internal clock with natural circadian rhythms. When your body is in sync with these rhythms, you're more likely to experience restorative sleep, which is crucial for cognitive function, memory consolidation, and emotional regulation. Quality sleep can significantly enhance your mental clarity and focus, making it easier to take on the day's challenges.

Another often-overlooked advantage of waking up early is the ability to complete complex or dreaded tasks before distractions creep in. If you start your day by tackling your most challenging tasks, you'll find that your mental energy remains high, and your sense of accomplishment can propel you forward. This early momentum sets a positive tone, making it easier to maintain focus throughout the day.

Furthermore, the early hours of the morning can be a time for self-reflection and assessment. This is an ideal period to review personal progress, set intentions, and align your actions with your long-term goals. Taking this time for introspection can provide a clear roadmap for your day and your life, enhanced by the mental clarity that comes from waking up before the distractions and demands of the day begin.

It's also worth mentioning the psychological impact of waking up early. When you know you're starting your day ahead of most people, it can instill a sense of accomplishment and confidence. This psychological edge can sharpen your focus, making you more alert and receptive to the tasks at hand. Confidence in your ability to manage time and priorities can further enhance your mental clarity.

Finally, waking up early can improve your overall mental health, which directly impacts clarity and focus. The combination of adequate sleep, exercise, nutritious food, and a peaceful start to the day can reduce stress and anxiety levels. When your mental health is in good standing, you're naturally more focused and clear-headed. It's a holistic approach that encompasses not just the act of waking up early but the cumulative effects of positive habits that come with it.

In summary, waking up early offers a unique synergy of benefits that contribute to enhanced mental clarity and focus. From creating undisturbed time for deep work and planning to fostering habits that improve overall mental health, the advantages are manifold. For ambitious professionals and individuals looking to elevate their productivity and personal growth, embracing the early morning hours can be a transformative practice, paving the way for sustained success and well-being.

Chapter 3: Designing Your Perfect Morning

In crafting your ideal morning, the first step is to understand what drives you and aligns with your aspirations. Consider the goals that resonate most with your life vision—whether it's professional success, personal growth, or a harmonious blend of both. This clarity becomes the bedrock upon which your routine is built. Next, construct a sequence of activities that not only energize and inspire you but also set a productive tone for the day. Your routine should be bespoke to you, reflecting your unique needs and ambitions. From energizing exercises to moments of mindfulness, each component should serve a purpose and synergize to create a powerful start to your day. By intentionally designing your mornings, you lay the foundation for sustained productivity and well-being, transforming your aspirations into tangible realities.

Identifying Your Goals

When embarking on the journey to craft your ideal morning, the first step is to identify your goals. It's essential to understand what you want to achieve with your mornings because a clear sense of purpose can significantly enhance your motivation and consistency. Goals provide direction, and with the right goals, your morning routine can become a powerful tool for personal and professional growth.

Identifying your goals starts with a bit of introspection. Take some time to reflect on what matters most to you—both in the short term and the long term. Ask yourself key questions: What are my top priorities right now? What aspects of my life need more attention? Where do I see myself in the next year, five years, or ten years? These types of inquiries can help you zero in on goals that are meaningful and aligned with your vision for your future.

Everyone has different aspirations, and your morning routine should be personalized to support yours. For instance, if you're aiming to improve your physical health, you'll want to incorporate activities that promote fitness, such as morning workouts or yoga. On the other hand, if career advancement is your primary goal, dedicating time to skill-building or strategic planning might serve you better. The essence of identifying your goals lies in tailoring your routine to fit your unique journey.

It's also crucial to distinguish between different types of goals. Short-term goals, such as completing a specific project at work, often require a different kind of focus compared to long-term goals, like establishing a healthier lifestyle. Both are important, but they require varying levels of daily commitment and types of activities. By categorizing your goals, you can create a balanced morning routine that addresses immediate needs while also fostering long-term growth.

Your goals might also be multifaceted, spanning across various areas of your life: physical health, mental wellbeing, career, personal development, and relationships. To avoid being overwhelmed, start with a few core goals and gradually expand as you become more comfortable and effective with your routine. The goal here is not to pack your mornings with endless tasks, but to allocate time thoughtfully so that each goal gets the attention it deserves.

One effective method for goal identification is the SMART criteria—making sure your goals are Specific, Measurable, Achievable, Relevant, and Time-bound. This framework encourages clarity and feasibility, reducing the risk of setting abstract or overly ambitious goals that might lead to discouragement. For example, instead of setting a vague goal like "get fitter," you can aim for "run three miles every morning." The specificity and measurability of the goal make it easier to track progress and stay accountable.

Breaking down larger goals into smaller, manageable tasks can also be incredibly effective. If your long-term goal is to write a book, include morning writing sessions in your routine. By dedicating just thirty minutes each morning to writing, you'll make consistent progress without feeling overwhelmed by the enormity of the task. Small steps, taken consistently, pave the way for significant achievements over time.

It's important to periodically review and adjust your goals. Life is dynamic, and your priorities may shift. What seemed crucial six months ago might take a back seat to a new, more pressing goal. Regularly reassessing your goals ensures that your morning routine remains relevant and continues to serve your evolving aspirations. Don't be afraid to pivot and make changes; flexibility is key to maintaining a routine that's both effective and sustainable.

Moreover, aligning your goals with your core values can significantly boost your commitment and satisfaction. Core values are the fundamental beliefs that guide your actions and decisions. Whether it's integrity, creativity, or compassion, aligning your goals with your values can enhance your intrinsic motivation. For example, if personal growth is a core value, incorporating activities such as reading, meditation, or journaling can enrich your mornings and keep you engaged with your routine.

As you identify your goals, it's worth considering how they interact with and support each other. Synergistic goals can enhance each other's outcomes. For instance, a goal to improve physical fitness can positively affect mental clarity and productivity at work. Similarly, a goal to practice mindfulness can improve emotional resilience, benefiting both personal and professional relationships. Understanding these interconnections can help you design a more cohesive and rewarding morning routine.

Finally, communicating your goals to others can provide additional layers of accountability and support. Whether it's sharing with a partner, a mentor, or a friend, explaining your objectives and the reasons behind them can solidify your commitment. Moreover, discussing your goals can open up opportunities for others to join you in your journey, creating a supportive community that shares and celebrates each other's progress.

In summary, identifying your goals is a foundational step in designing your perfect morning. It requires introspection, categorization, and periodic reassessment. By setting SMART goals, breaking down larger objectives into smaller tasks, aligning your goals with your core values, and seeking both synergy and support, you can create a morning routine that is not only productive but also deeply satisfying. This thoughtful approach ensures that each morning becomes a step forward on the path to achieving your dreams and aspirations.

Creating a Custom Routine

Crafting a morning routine that's tailored specifically to you can be a game-changer. It's not just about copying someone else's schedule; it's about creating something that fits your unique lifestyle, personality, and goals. So let's dive into the nitty-gritty of how you can build your own custom routine to kickstart your mornings and set yourself up for success.

First, it's crucial to identify your core goals. What do you want to achieve by revamping your mornings? Maybe you're aiming for better productivity, more energy, or a quieter mind. Whatever it is, be clear and specific about your objectives. This clarity will guide you as you design a routine that serves your purpose.

Next, think about the activities that align with these goals. If boosting productivity is your aim, activities such as planning your day or tackling a challenging task first thing might be beneficial. If your focus is on mental well-being, meditation or journaling could be key components. Write down a list of potential activities and prioritize them.

Not all of us are the same, and that's what makes creating a customized routine so vital. Consider your personal preferences and natural rhythms. Are you a morning person, or do you struggle to get out of bed? Tailor your routine to fit your energy levels and mood at different times of the morning. If you're not naturally a morning person, start with small, manageable changes and gradually build up.

Once you've got a list of activities, it's time to experiment. Pick a few and incorporate them into your morning. Notice how you feel and how it impacts your day. Keep what works and ditch what doesn't. The idea is to be flexible and open to modification. After all, the perfect routine is a moving target; it evolves as you do.

CHAPTER 3: DESIGNING YOUR PERFECT MORNING

One powerful tool in your arsenal is the concept of habit stacking. This involves linking new habits to existing ones, making it easier to remember and execute them. For example, if you want to start journalizing, you might decide to do it right after making your bed. Over time, these linked habits become second nature, making your routine more seamless and intuitive.

Structure is essential, but so is variety. Routines can become monotonous if they don't engage you on multiple levels. Mix things up to keep them interesting. Maybe alternate between different types of workouts or change up your breakfast menu from time to time. Small variations can keep you motivated and excited about your mornings.

Let's not overlook the importance of setting realistic expectations. Life is unpredictable, and some mornings won't go as planned. When building your routine, include some buffer time for unexpected events. The goal is consistency, not perfection. It's better to have a 70% effective routine that you stick to than a 100% effective one that you give up on after a week.

Creating a custom routine is also about aligning with your broader life goals. Make sure your morning activities are not only fulfilling immediate needs but also contributing to long-term aspirations. This could be personal development activities like reading a chapter of a book, working on a new skill, or even practicing a hobby.

Don't forget to measure your progress. Keep a journal or log to track how your routine impacts your productivity, mood, and overall well-being. This will give you valuable insights and help you tweak your routine for even better results. Periodic reflection can provide the adjustments needed to keep your routine relevant and effective.

The environment plays a crucial role in the success of your morning routine. Create a space that is conducive to the activities you've chosen. Whether it's a quiet corner for meditation or a fully stocked kitchen for a nutritious breakfast, your environment should support and enhance your routine, not detract from it.

Lastly, be kind to yourself. Building a custom routine takes time and patience. Don't get discouraged if you don't see immediate results. Remember, every small step you take is progress, and over time these small steps will accumulate into significant changes.

In essence, creating a custom routine is about designing a morning that sets you up for the day you want to have. It's an investment in yourself that, when thoughtfully crafted and consistently applied, can yield incredible dividends in terms of productivity, well-being, and personal growth. So go ahead, design your perfect morning and take charge of your day.

Chapter 4: The Power of Consistency

The key to unlocking the full potential of your morning routine lies in the power of consistency. It's not just about crafting the perfect set of activities to kickstart your day, but about repeating them with unwavering regularity. By doing so, you turn one-off actions into habits, and these habits become the bedrock of your daily success. Think of each morning as an opportunity to reinforce your goals and set a positive tone for the rest of the day. Consistency helps cement those small actions into your subconscious, making them second nature. When challenges impede your progress, consistency becomes your ally, helping you weather obstacles and stay on track. Embrace the power of showing up each day, and watch as your productivity, mental clarity, and overall well-being begin to soar.

Building Habits

Building habits is the cornerstone of creating a consistent and impactful morning routine. It's the secret sauce that can turn your mornings from chaotic to calm, from lethargic to lively. But let's be clear: building habits isn't a magic trick. It requires time, patience, and a touch of resilience. If you can commit to the process, though, the rewards are enormous.

Ever wondered why some people seem to have it all together while you struggle to get through your first cup of coffee? Often, it boils down to the habits they've built and the consistency they've maintained. Establishing a morning habit isn't just about waking up early but creating a series of small, beneficial practices that set a positive tone for the day.

The first step to building any habit is understanding what you want to achieve. Maybe it's to feel more energized, be more productive, or perhaps you want to cultivate a sense of calmness to counteract a stressful job. Identifying your 'why' gives meaning to the habits you're trying to build and keeps you motivated when the initial excitement wears off.

Next, start small. It's tempting to overhaul your entire routine overnight, but that approach often leads to burnout. Instead, focus on one small change at a time. If your goal is to exercise in the morning, begin with just five minutes. Once that five minutes becomes second nature, gradually increase the duration. The key is to make the habit so small it's almost impossible to fail.

Let's talk about triggers. Habits are often built around triggers, which are cues that prompt you to perform a specific action. For instance, setting your workout clothes beside your bed can serve as a visual reminder to exercise in the morning. These triggers help you transition from the intention of doing something to actually doing it. They're like the little nudge you need to get started.

Consistency is another critical component. It's not enough to perform an action a few times and expect it to stick. Research suggests that it takes an average of 66 days for a new habit to become automatic. This timeline can vary depending on the individual and the complexity of the habit, but the takeaway is clear: consistency is crucial. Even if you miss a day, don't beat yourself up. Jump back in the next day and keep going.

Accountability can also play a significant role in habit formation. Sharing your goals with a friend or joining a group with similar objectives can provide the external motivation you need. Knowing that someone else is keeping an eye on your progress can push you to stay committed, even on days when your motivation is lacking.

Rewards shouldn't be overlooked either. While the long-term benefits of a new habit can be rewarding, immediate rewards can keep you motivated. Treat yourself to something small when you complete your morning routine, whether it's a delicious breakfast, a few minutes of your favorite music, or even a sticker on a calendar. These small rewards reinforce the habit and

CHAPTER 4: THE POWER OF CONSISTENCY

make it more enjoyable.

Another essential element in building habits is self-compassion. Understand that setbacks are a natural part of the process. Instead of viewing them as failures, see them as learning experiences. What triggered the setback? How can you prevent it in the future? This reflective approach not only helps you get back on track but also makes the habit-forming journey less stressful.

Visualization can also be a powerful tool. Mentally rehearsing your new habit can make it easier to perform in real life. Spend a few minutes each day visualizing yourself successfully completing your morning routine. This exercise trains your brain to recognize the new habit as part of your identity, making it easier to adopt in real life.

It's also helpful to track your progress. Keeping a habit journal or using an app to monitor your advancements can give you insights into what works and what doesn't. When you see a string of successful days, it creates a sense of accomplishment and motivates you to keep going.

Lastly, it's important to periodically reassess your habits. What worked for you a month ago might not be effective now. Life circumstances change, new challenges arise, and what once felt beneficial might start to feel burdensome. Adjusting your habits to fit your current lifestyle ensures they remain effective and sustainable.

In conclusion, building habits is an art that involves a series of thoughtful, consistent actions. Start small, use triggers, stay accountable, and reward yourself. Embrace setbacks with a growth mindset and continually assess your progress. When done correctly, these habits can transform your mornings and, by extension, your entire day. Taking the time to cultivate positive habits is an investment in your future self—a future where you wake up each day ready to conquer whatever comes your way.

Overcoming Obstacles

Consistency is a powerful force, yet maintaining it can be one of the most challenging aspects of any routine. It's easy to start strong, but as days turn into weeks, the initial enthusiasm can wane. Understanding this, and knowing how to overcome the obstacles that threaten to derail your morning routine, is crucial for sustained success.

The first obstacle many people face is the temptation to stay in bed when the alarm goes off. Your bed is warm and comfortable, and the pull to hit the snooze button can be irresistible. However, this is where discipline comes into play. One strategy to combat this is to place your alarm across the room, forcing you to physically get out of bed to turn it off. This physical movement can often be enough to shake off the initial drowsiness and kickstart your day.

Another prevalent challenge is inconsistency due to an irregular sleep schedule. Going to bed at a different time each night disrupts your body's natural rhythm, making it harder to wake up at the same time each morning. To overcome this, establish a set bedtime and stick to it, even on weekends. This not only makes waking up easier but also ensures you're getting sufficient rest.

Distractions also pose a significant threat to maintaining a consistent morning routine. From the lure of checking your phone first thing in the morning to unexpected demands from work or family, distractions can easily throw off your schedule. One effective method to tackle this is to create a morning "bubble" – a dedicated period where you focus solely on your routine without outside interference. Turn off notifications, communicate boundaries to those around you, and create a space where distractions are minimized.

There's also the obstacle of lack of motivation. Some mornings, the bed feels harder to leave, and the routine feels like a burden rather than a benefit. To combat this, remind yourself of your 'why.' Why did you start this routine in the first place? Was it to achieve a particular goal or to feel a certain way? Keeping a journal where you write down these reasons can serve as a powerful motivator on days when your drive is low.

Overwhelm can be another major hurdle. Trying to implement too many changes at once can feel daunting and can lead to burnout. The key is to start small. Introduce one new habit at a time and gradually build on it. This makes the adjustment period more manageable and allows each new habit to become ingrained before adding another component to your morning routine.

CHAPTER 4: THE POWER OF CONSISTENCY

Physical and mental fatigue can also disrupt consistency. If you're not getting enough rest or are feeling mentally drained, it's important to listen to your body. However, distinguish between genuine fatigue and habitual laziness. If you find that lack of sleep is a constant issue, revisit your evening routine to see where improvements can be made. Are you exposing yourself to too much blue light before bed? Is your sleep environment conducive to rest? Small adjustments can make significant differences.

Another common obstacle is the perception of not having enough time. Many people believe their mornings are too short to fit in a consistent routine. However, the solution often lies in better time management and prioritization. Reevaluate your morning tasks and eliminate or delegate non-essential activities. Sometimes, setting your alarm even 15 minutes earlier can provide the space you need to complete your routine without feeling rushed.

Stress and anxiety can also be disruptors. Life is filled with unexpected events that can throw off your routine. When stress levels are high, it's easy to abandon your morning habits. This is where resilience comes into play. Building a routine that includes stress-reduction techniques such as meditation, deep breathing exercises, or journaling can help mitigate these effects. Additionally, acknowledging that some days won't go as planned and being kind to yourself during these times is essential. The key is to get back on track as soon as possible.

It's also important to address the role of self-doubt. Many people believe they aren't capable of maintaining a consistent routine due to past failures. This mindset can be a self-fulfilling prophecy. Instead, adopt a growth mindset: understand that failure is part of the learning process, and each setback is an opportunity to learn and improve. Celebrate small victories along the way to build your confidence and create positive reinforcement.

Accountability can be a powerful tool to overcome many of these obstacles. Share your goals with a friend or family member who can check in with you regularly. Join a community or group with similar goals where you can share your struggles and victories. The sense of belonging and mutual support can be incredibly motivating and help keep you on track.

Finally, integrating flexibility into your routine is essential. Life is unpredictable, and a rigid routine can sometimes do more harm than good. Allow yourself some leeway. If you miss a day or need to adjust your routine due to unforeseen circumstances, it's not the end of the world. What's more important is the overall pattern of consistency rather than perfection. Consistency isn't about doing the same thing every single day without fail; it's about building a habit that withstands the test of time and adapts to life's changes.

In essence, overcoming obstacles in your morning routine is about preparation, adaptation, and resilience. It's about understanding that the road to consistency is not a straight path but a journey with ups and downs. Equip yourself with strategies to handle the inevitable challenges, and learn to embrace the process. Success lies not in never failing but in rising each time you fall. With persistence and the right mindset, the power of consistency can transform your mornings and, ultimately, your life.

Chapter 5: Nutrition and Hydration

To kickstart your day with vigor and clarity, it's vital to pay attention to your nutrition and hydration. Factors like a well-balanced breakfast and consistent fluid intake play pivotal roles in both physical energy levels and cognitive function. Imagine your body as a finely-tuned machine: the right fuel in the morning can turbocharge your productivity, while proper hydration ensures all systems are running smoothly. Opt for breakfasts rich in proteins, healthy fats, and complex carbohydrates, which release energy steadily throughout the day. Simultaneously, don't underestimate the power of water. Adequate hydration impacts everything from your mood to your ability to focus on those crucial morning tasks. By prioritizing what you eat and drink in the early hours, you create a foundation strong enough to support the demands of an ambitious, goal-oriented lifestyle.

The Best Breakfasts for Energy

Starting your day with the right breakfast can be a game-changer when it comes to maintaining high energy levels throughout the day. Entering the world of nutritious breakfasts might feel overwhelming, but the rewards of getting it right are immense. Imagine rolling into your first meeting of the day feeling focused, lively, and ready to tackle any challenge that comes your way. That's the power of a well-balanced breakfast!

So, what exactly makes a breakfast energizing? First and foremost, it's all about balance—balancing macronutrients (carbohydrates, proteins, and fats) and incorporating micronutrients (vitamins and minerals). A nutritious breakfast should include a good mix of complex carbohydrates, lean proteins, and healthy fats. This combo ensures a slow release of energy, keeping those hunger pangs at bay and preventing energy crashes.

Complex carbohydrates are your go-to for sustained energy. Foods like whole grains, fruits, and vegetables are excellent sources. For instance, starting your day with a bowl of oatmeal topped with fresh berries and a drizzle of honey not only satisfies your sweet tooth but also provides fiber and antioxidants. The fiber helps with digestion and keeps you feeling full longer, allowing for a gradual release of glucose into the bloodstream—your primary energy source.

Proteins are crucial for muscle repair and growth, but they also play a significant role in keeping you alert. Eggs are often heralded as breakfast champions for good reasons. They're packed with high-quality protein and essential nutrients like choline, which supports brain health. Imagine scrambling some eggs with spinach and tomatoes, giving you a nutrient-packed start that boosts both physical and mental energy.

Healthy fats—often demonized in outdated dietary advice—are essential for brain function and overall cellular health. Avocados, nuts, and seeds are fantastic sources of healthy fats. Consider spreading some mashed avocado on a slice of whole-grain toast and sprinkling it with chia seeds for an energizing, nutrient-dense breakfast option. It's delightful, satiating, and provides unsaturated fats that support heart health and cognitive function.

Of course, breakfast isn't merely about the macronutrients. Micronutrients, though needed in lesser quantities, play indispensable roles in maintaining energy levels. For example, a smoothie incorporating spinach, banana, almond milk, and a dash of spirulina powder can offer a punch of vitamins and minerals. The iron from spinach helps in producing red blood cells, which transport oxygen throughout your body, boosting both energy and alertness.

One often-overlooked aspect of an energizing breakfast is hydration. Dehydration, even at mild levels, can lead to fatigue and sluggishness. Starting your day with a glass of water or a hydrating beverage like coconut water can set a positive tone for the day. Herbal teas, such as peppermint or ginger, not only hydrate but also have invigorating properties that can enhance your morning vitality.

Speaking of smoothies, they deserve special mention. Smoothies are versatile and can be tailored to your nutritional needs. A well-crafted smoothie can serve as a full meal, combining fruits, vegetables, protein sources like Greek yogurt or protein powder, and healthy fats such as almond butter or flaxseeds. The key is to avoid loading your smoothie with too many sugary fruits and instead aim for a balance that provides sustained energy.

For those who prefer something with a bit more chew, whole-grain options like quinoa bowls are excellent. Quinoa is a complete protein, meaning it contains all nine essential amino acids that our bodies can't produce on their own. Combine cooked quinoa with sautéed vegetables and a poached egg for a savory breakfast bowl. This not only keeps your taste buds interested but also ensures you get a wide range of nutrients.

If you have a sweet tooth, consider making chia pudding the night before. Chia seeds are an excellent source of omega-3 fatty acids, fiber, and protein. Soaking them overnight in almond milk creates a pudding-like texture. In the morning, layer this chia pudding with fresh fruits and a handful of nuts. It's a delightful, nutrient-packed breakfast that's ready to go when you are.

Let's not forget traditional yet often overlooked fermented foods. Greek yogurt or kefir offers probiotics that foster a healthy gut. A balanced gut can improve nutrient absorption, which is crucial for maintaining energy. Pair them with some granola and berries for a breakfast that's as tasty as it is functional.

While considering these varied options, remember that skipping breakfast can be a major pitfall. Professionals often excuse themselves from breakfast citing tight schedules, but the resulting energy dips and impaired focus can be counterproductive. If time is a constraint, prepare overnight oats in a jar or grab a couple of boiled eggs and a piece of fruit—quick, easy, and immensely beneficial.

Developing a breakfast routine that works for you might involve some initial experimentation. Pay attention to how different foods make you feel throughout the morning. Keep a journal to note what sustains your energy best and what leaves you feeling sluggish. This self-awareness will lead you to a personalized breakfast blueprint that fits seamlessly into your morning routine and sets you up for success.

In summing up, the importance of a well-balanced breakfast is undeniable in the quest for high energy and productivity. Embrace the possibilities, diversify your choices, and make breakfast an indispensable part of your morning regimen. The right breakfast does more than just curb hunger—it fortifies you, mentally and physically, to face the day's challenges with vigor.

Hydration Tips

Wake up. Hydrate. Unlock your full potential. This motto can transform your mornings and your entire day. While many of us focus on what we eat for breakfast or the exercise routines we follow, we often overlook the simple yet powerful act of proper hydration. It's not just about quenching your thirst; it's about fueling your body and mind for optimum performance.

Let's start with the facts. Overnight, your body loses water through breath and perspiration. By the time you wake up, you're already in a state of mild dehydration. This can affect your cognitive functions, energy levels, and overall mood. So, the first actionable tip is to drink a glass of water as soon as you get up. It doesn't have to be plain; a splash of lemon or a teaspoon of apple cider vinegar can make it more palatable and help with your digestive system, too.

But it's not enough to just gulp down water first thing in the morning. Hydration is a continuous process that requires mindful attention throughout the day. Keep a bottle of water or an easy-to-access water source handy. Set reminders if you must. Many of us are great at starting the day with healthy intentions but get so caught up in our tasks that we forget to keep hydrated.

Here's another crucial point: Not all liquids are created equal. Coffee and caffeinated teas are diuretics, which means they can lead to increased urination and, ultimately, dehydration. This doesn't mean you have to give up your morning coffee. Just balance it out by drinking a glass of water for each cup of coffee you consume.

CHAPTER 5: NUTRITION AND HYDRATION

Electrolytes play a significant role in hydration, especially if you're incorporating exercise into your morning routine. Sweating causes you to lose not just water but also essential minerals like sodium, potassium, and magnesium. Consider drinking an electrolyte-rich beverage post-workout to replenish these vital nutrients. You can choose a commercial sports drink or, better yet, make your own by mixing water with a pinch of Himalayan salt and a squeeze of lemon.

Another way to stay hydrated is through your diet. Foods with high water content, such as cucumbers, oranges, and watermelon, contribute to your overall hydration. Including them in your breakfast or as snacks can make a substantial difference. Remember, fruits and vegetables are not just hydration boosters; they also come packed with fibers, vitamins, and antioxidants that serve as rewards for your entire body.

If you find it challenging to drink enough water, make it interesting! Infuse your water with herbs like mint, basil, or rosemary. Add slices of fruit like strawberries, kiwis, or citrus. This not only makes the water more flavorful but can also provide additional vitamins and minerals.

Keep in mind that the environment you're in affects your body's need for water. You'll need more hydration during hot and humid days than in cooler climates. Similarly, indoor conditions, especially heated or air-conditioned spaces, can contribute to dehydration faster than you might expect. Always adjust your water intake to align with your environment.

Understanding your body's signals is also vital. Thirst is an indicator, but often by the time you feel thirsty, you're already starting to dehydrate. Other signs to look out for include dark-colored urine, dry mouth, fatigue, and dizziness. Be proactive about your hydration rather than reactive.

Now, let's address a common concern - how much water should you actually drink? The "8x8" rule, which advocates for eight 8-ounce glasses of water a day, is a good starting point. However, individual needs can vary based on weight, activity level, and other health conditions. A more personalized approach involves drinking half your body weight in ounces of water each day. For instance, if you weigh 150 pounds, aim for 75 ounces of water.

For those who are busy professionals, syncing hydration with your schedule can work wonders. Break your day into segments and associate each segment with a hydration checkpoint. For example, drink a glass of water upon waking, another mid-morning, one with lunch, one mid-afternoon, one with dinner, and another in the evening. Making it a part of your routine ensures you stay adequately hydrated without having to think about it constantly.

The impact of staying well-hydrated goes beyond just physical wellbeing. Mentally, you'll find increased clarity and focus. Schools of cognitive research suggest that even mild dehydration can impair cognitive functions such as attention, memory, and motor coordination. In essence, staying hydrated can be a mental productivity hack.

Enthusiasts of personal growth and productivity often measure their progress through key performance indicators, and hydration should be one of them. You can track your daily water intake using various apps or even a simple handwritten log. Consistent monitoring can help you identify patterns and make necessary adjustments to your routine.

Lastly, let's talk about when it's particularly important to be mindful of your hydration – during travel, whether it's for work or leisure. Flights can be especially dehydrating due to low humidity levels in the cabin. Make a habit of bringing an empty, reusable water bottle through security and fill it up before you board. Sip water regularly throughout your journey to counteract the dry cabin air.

The benefits of proper hydration are endless, impacting virtually every system in your body. By making it a non-negotiable part of your morning routine, you set the stage for a day that's energized, focused, and productive. Hydration is a simple, actionable tip that can have profound effects on your overall wellbeing and performance.

This small but significant habit doesn't require much effort, but the rewards are substantial. As you craft your perfect morning routine, never underestimate the power of a glass of water. It's one of the simplest yet most effective ways to take control of your day right from the very start.

Chapter 6: Exercise and Movement

Embracing morning exercise can be a game-changer for ambitious professionals and individuals seeking to amplify their productivity and personal growth. Starting your day with movement doesn't just invigorate your body; it primes your mind for the challenges ahead. Whether it's a brisk run, a calming yoga session, or an energizing stretch routine, morning workouts release endorphins, enhance mental clarity, and set a positive tone for the day. Imagine starting your morning with a burst of energy that fuels not just your muscles, but also your determination and focus. By incorporating consistent physical activity into your routine, you'll not only boost your physical health but also sharpen your mental acuity, making you better equipped to tackle the tasks of the day. So, lace up those sneakers, roll out that yoga mat, and move towards a more productive and fulfilling life.

Morning Workouts

Let's dive into one of the most impactful pieces of a morning routine: morning workouts. Starting your day with physical activity can profoundly shape the rest of your day, setting the tone for productivity and positivity. Whether you're a seasoned athlete or someone who barely knows the difference between a dumbbell and a barbell, incorporating a morning workout into your daily routine can offer incredible physical and mental health benefits.

First and foremost, morning workouts ignite your metabolism. When you exercise early, you're essentially jumpstarting your body's engine, giving it a reason to burn calories more efficiently throughout the day. This boost can be a game-changer for those aiming to get fitter, lose weight, or maintain a healthy body composition. The science behind this is pretty straightforward: morning exercise increases your metabolic rate, meaning your body will continue to burn calories at a higher rate, even when you're not working out.

Beyond the metabolic advantages, morning workouts also foster mental clarity. Physical activity stimulates the release of endorphins, often dubbed as "feel-good hormones." These endorphins can elevate your mood and provide a sense of accomplishment that reverberates through the rest of your activities. Think of it as giving your brain a natural shot of espresso without the jitters. Additionally, studies have shown that exercise can help improve cognitive function, enhancing focus and problem-solving skills—tools essential for any ambitious professional.

A key element to successful morning workouts lies in variety and choosing what you enjoy. Whether it's a high-intensity interval training (HIIT) session, a peaceful run in the park, or a calming yoga routine, it's crucial to find an exercise that you look forward to. This way, you're more likely to stick with it. Mixing up your workouts can also keep things interesting and ensure that you're working different muscle groups, preventing monotony and potential injuries. Consistency doesn't mean doing the same thing every day; it means showing up for yourself regularly.

Another essential aspect to consider is preparation. Laying out your workout clothes the night before can eliminate decisions in the morning and can give you an extra push to actually get moving. Setting up your water bottle, mat, and any other equipment you might need ensures you're ready to dive in without any excuses.

It's also beneficial to match your workouts to your goals and energy levels. For those mornings when you're bursting with energy, go for a vigorous cardio workout or lift some weights. On days when you feel less motivated, a gentler activity like stretching or yoga can still keep you in the habit of moving your body, without feeling overwhelming.

Speaking of energy levels, fueling your body properly is vital. A light snack before working out can provide the necessary energy if you're feeling sluggish.

CHAPTER 6: EXERCISE AND MOVEMENT

Something as simple as a banana or a small handful of nuts can make a big difference. Post-workout, focus on replenishing your body with a balanced meal that includes protein, carbohydrates, and healthy fats to aid recovery and sustain your energy throughout the day.

For those juggling busy schedules, time-efficient workouts can be a lifesaver. High-Intensity Interval Training (HIIT) is especially effective because it allows you to get the most out of a short period of time. These workouts typically involve bursts of intense activity followed by short rest periods, maximizing calorie burn and cardiovascular benefits. A 20-minute HIIT session can be just as, if not more, effective than a longer, moderate-intensity workout.

Accountability is another powerful motivator. Finding a workout buddy or joining a morning exercise group can create a sense of community and mutual encouragement. Even if you prefer working out alone, sharing your goals and progress with a friend or a virtual community can hold you accountable and provide extra motivation to roll out of bed on those tougher mornings.

As with any new habit, the initial phase will involve a period of adjustment. It's essential to listen to your body and avoid pushing yourself to the point of burnout or injury. Start slow, maybe two or three times a week, and gradually increase the frequency as your body adapts. The goal is to make morning workouts a sustainable and enjoyable part of your lifestyle, not a fleeting attempt at getting fit.

Space is equally important in setting the stage for effective morning workouts. If you're working out at home, designate a specific area where you can lay out your mat and equipment, free from distractions. A quiet, organized space can make your workouts feel more intentional and less like an afterthought. If you prefer going to a gym, selecting one close to your home can make it easier to stick to your routine. The less friction between you and your workout, the better.

On a deeper level, morning workouts teach us the art of prioritization and discipline. When you commit to exercising first thing in the morning, you're essentially telling yourself that your health and wellbeing come first. This act of self-care can ripple into other areas of your life, fostering a mindset of growth and improvement.

The beauty of morning workouts lies in their adaptability. If running isn't your thing, perhaps you'd enjoy a bike ride or a dance class. If high-intensity workouts are too taxing, a brisk walk or a swim might suit you better. The type of exercise matters less than the act of consistently moving your body in the morning. Evaluate your preferences, and don't be afraid to experiment until you find what feels right for you.

When integrated thoughtfully into your morning routine, workouts become more than just a chore—they become a cornerstone of a productive and fulfilling day. They offer a moment of solitude and self-reflection, a time to connect with your body and prepare your mind for the challenges ahead. As you feel your body growing stronger, your mind will follow, sharpening your focus and enhancing your resilience.

So, take this as your invitation to start moving in the mornings. From the smallest stretch to the most intense workout, every bit contributes to a larger picture of health, happiness, and productivity. Embrace the journey, and let your mornings become a testament to your commitment to your best self.

Stretching and Yoga Practices

Incorporating stretching and yoga into your morning routine can be a game-changer for enhancing productivity and overall well-being. These practices not only prepare your body physically for the day ahead but also set a positive, mindful tone that can ripple through your entire day. Yoga and stretching are accessible to everyone, regardless of fitness level, and can be tailored to meet individual needs. The effects are not just limited to physical flexibility; they also extend to mental clarity and emotional resilience.

Let's start with the physical aspects. Stretching in the morning helps to relieve muscle stiffness accumulated during sleep. Stretching can boost your circulation, waking up your muscles and increasing blood flow to your brain. This can make you feel more alert and focused, setting a productive tone from the get-go. Simple movements like neck rolls, shoulder shrugs, and calf stretches can make a world of difference. You don't need to spend hours on this; even a five-minute routine can kickstart your day effectively.

Transitioning to yoga, this ancient practice does more than just stretch your muscles; it incorporates elements of strength training, balance, and mindful breathing. A well-rounded yoga session can rejuvenate your body and mind, providing a serene yet invigorating start to your day. Poses like the Forward Fold can release your lower back and hamstrings, while the Cat-Cow stretch can mobilize your spine. If you're new to yoga, starting with a guided session via a mobile app or online video can offer you the structure you need.

Mentally, stretching and yoga also cultivate mindfulness. The act of stretching itself can be a meditative experience if done consciously. Focus on how your muscles feel as they elongate and contract. This brings your awareness to the present moment, a foundational element of mindfulness. Over time, you'll find that this mindfulness starts to extend into other parts of your day, helping you make more deliberate, thoughtful decisions.

Breathing is an integral part of yoga, and mastering it can benefit your mental clarity. Practices like Pranayama involve controlled breathing exercises that can reduce stress and increase focus. Try starting with simple breathing exercises: inhale deeply through your nose for a count of four, hold for four, then exhale through your mouth for a count of four. This pattern can help to center your mind and create a sense of calm, readiness for your day.

Aside from the individual benefits, incorporating stretching and yoga into your morning routine can foster a sense of accomplishment early in the day. Completing a routine gives you a sense of achievement, boosting your motivation for other tasks. It's an empowering feeling, knowing you've already done something beneficial for your body and mind before most people have even started their day.

For those with demanding schedules, the idea of adding another activity can seem overwhelming. However, the beauty of stretching and yoga lies in their flexibility. You don't need an hour-long session to reap the benefits. A concise, 10-minute routine can be just as effective. Focus on quality over quantity. The key is consistency; regular practice will yield far better results than sporadic, lengthy sessions.

There's also a social aspect to consider. Engaging in group yoga sessions, whether in-person or virtually, can add another layer to your practice. This shared experience can offer a sense of community and accountability. You might feel more encouraged to stick with your routine when you know others are doing it alongside you. Plus, you can exchange tips and experiences, enriching your practice and possibly discovering new routines that work best for you.

Now, let's talk about adaptability. Your stretching and yoga practices can evolve with you. As you grow more comfortable with certain stretches or poses, you can graduate to more advanced techniques. Your routine should never feel stale or stagnant; aim to keep it dynamic and responsive to your body's needs. Seasons change, life circumstances shift, but your commitment to this practice can remain a constant anchor.

To sum it up, the inclusion of stretching and yoga in your morning routine has multifaceted benefits. Physically, they prepare your body for the day, improve flexibility, and enhance circulation. Mentally, they focus your mind, promote mindfulness, and reduce stress. Emotionally, they provide a sense of accomplishment and well-being. Even a brief, consistent morning practice can have lasting effects on your productivity and overall happiness.

In embracing these practices, you're not just adding another task to your morning; you're investing in your health and productivity. Stretching and yoga offer a holistic approach to starting your day, harmonizing body, mind, and spirit. These moments of deliberate movement set a positive tone, positioning you to tackle your day's challenges with clarity and resilience.

So, as you design your perfect morning routine, consider the enduring benefits these ancient practices bring. With consistency and mindfulness, stretching and yoga can become the cornerstone of a transformative morning, propelling you towards a day of heightened productivity and well-being. Remember, the journey to personal growth is a marathon, and every stretch and pose brings you one breath closer to your best self.

Chapter 7: Mental and Emotional Wellbeing

Enhancing mental and emotional wellbeing is crucial for maximizing the benefits of your morning routine. By starting your day with practices that center and ground your mind, you create a strong foundation for sustained productivity and personal growth. Incorporating activities like meditation and journaling helps you clear mental clutter, reduce stress, and set a positive tone for the day ahead. Meditation practices, even if brief, can foster mindfulness and focus, while journaling provides an outlet for introspection and emotional release. Prioritizing your mental and emotional health in the morning empowers you to navigate daily challenges with greater resilience and clarity, transforming your entire day into a series of conscious, purposeful actions.

Meditation Practices

Meditation can be a transformative component of your morning routine, setting the right tone for the day ahead. It's a practice that dates back thousands of years, yet it's more relevant than ever in our modern, fast-paced lives. For ambitious professionals aiming to boost productivity and personal growth, meditation offers a serene start that sharpens focus, enhances emotional wellbeing, and reduces stress.

The beauty of meditation is its simplicity. You don't need a fancy setup or a ton of time; even a few minutes of mindful breathing can make a world of difference. To get started, choose a quiet space where you can sit comfortably. Close your eyes, take deep breaths, and focus on the rise and fall of your chest. This basic practice, known as mindfulness meditation, helps clear the mental clutter, allowing you to start the day with a clean slate.

Consistency is critical here. Like building any other habit, the benefits of meditation amplify over time. Initially, you might feel restless or find your mind wandering. That's perfectly natural. The key is to gently guide your focus back to your breath or a chosen mantra whenever you notice it straying. Over days and weeks, you'll likely notice a shift—a newfound calmness and clarity that carries through the rest of your activities.

Incorporating meditation into your morning routine requires intentionality. Here are some tips to help you make it stick:

- **Start Small:** Begin with just five minutes a day to avoid feeling overwhelmed. Gradually increase the duration as you become more comfortable.
- **Set a Specific Time:** Timing can help anchor the habit. Many find right after waking up works best, but tailor it to your schedule.
- **Create a Ritual:** Light a candle, play calming music, or use essential oils to signal to your brain that it's time to meditate.
- **Use Guided Meditations:** Apps like Headspace or Calm offer structured sessions that can guide you through the process.

Beyond these basics, you can explore various meditation styles to keep things interesting and find what resonates most with you. Some might prefer transcendental meditation, which involves silently repeating a mantra. Others might lean towards guided imagery, where a narrator leads you through a series of relaxing and transformative visualizations.

Another powerful practice is loving-kindness meditation. It's particularly beneficial for those struggling with negative self-talk or interpersonal conflicts. This involves directing positive thoughts and well-wishes towards yourself and others, fostering a sense of universal compassion and empathy. Start by silently saying phrases like "May I be happy," "May I be healthy," and then extend those wishes to loved ones, acquaintances, and even difficult individuals in your life.

Breathwork is another form of meditation that's worth exploring. Techniques like diaphragmatic breathing, or the more advanced Wim Hof Method, can help enhance mental clarity and physical energy. By focusing on your breath, you activate the parasympathetic nervous system, which can reduce stress and promote a state of calm readiness. Imagine starting your day with a powerful yet peaceful mindset, ready to tackle any challenge that comes your way.

Integrating meditation into your morning routine isn't just about mental health—it can also have profound effects on your physical wellbeing. Studies show that regular meditation can lower blood pressure, improve sleep, and even boost your immune system. For the ambitious professional, this means fewer sick days, better energy levels, and a reduced risk of burnout.

It's helpful to keep a journal to track your meditation experiences. Note how you felt before and after each session, any thoughts or insights that arose, and any changes you're noticing over time. This not only helps in maintaining consistency but also gives tangible evidence of progress, reinforcing your commitment to the practice.

Now, let's dive a little deeper into specific meditation practices that can be particularly effective for enhancing productivity and emotional wellbeing:

1. **Mindfulness Meditation:** Focus on your breath, body scans, or the sounds around you. This practice enhances awareness and presence, pivotal for a productive day.
2. **Transcendental Meditation:** Involves repeating a specific mantra to transcend ordinary thought patterns, promoting deep rest and relaxation.
3. **Body Scan Meditation:** Gradually direct your attention through various parts of your body, releasing tension and fostering a sense of integrated wellbeing.
4. **Zen Meditation (Zazen):** A traditional practice involving seated meditation and focusing on one's breathing and posture to cultivate deep

mindfulness.

Ultimately, the best meditation practice is the one that feels right for you. It might take some experimentation to find the perfect fit, but the time invested in discovering your ideal routine will pay off immensely. Don't be discouraged by a busy mind or initial discomfort—these are just steps on the path to greater mental and emotional freedom.

Meditation is like a reset button for your brain. For professionals immersed in hectic schedules, this practice offers a rare space to breathe, reflect, and reconnect with your inner self. Embrace it as an essential part of your morning routine, and watch as your days become more centered, focused, and aligned with your true potential.

Start tomorrow. Set aside a few minutes and immerse yourself in the stillness. Allow it to become your sanctuary before the chaos of the day erupts. As you build this habit, you'll find that this simple practice can significantly elevate both your personal and professional life.

So, take a deep breath, close your eyes, and start your journey inward. The path to enhanced wellbeing and productivity lies within you, waiting to be unlocked each morning.

Journaling for Clarity

It's often said that the mind is a powerful tool. Yet, despite its capabilities, clarity can still elude us. One way to harness this mental prowess and direct it toward productive and clear thinking is through journaling. More than just writing on a page, journaling is about creating a dialogue with yourself. It's about setting aside a dedicated time, typically in the morning, to transfer your thoughts, feelings, and plans onto paper. This act can work wonders for mental and emotional wellbeing by providing a structured outlet for reflection and intention setting.

When you wake up in the morning, your mind is fresh, free from the clutter of the past day's events. This is the perfect time to engage in journaling. By jotting down your thoughts, you essentially perform a mental sweep, capturing stray ideas, anxieties, and ambitions. This practice not only provides a sense of relief but also allows you to start your day with a clean mental slate.

To dive into the practice of journaling, you don't need to be a seasoned writer. In fact, some of the most impactful journaling sessions come from raw, unfiltered thoughts. The goal is not to produce a polished piece of writing but to create an honest account of your inner dialogue. Consider this: how often do you have a conversation with yourself? If the answer is seldom, journaling can become that much-needed conversation.

A common method of journaling is the "stream of consciousness" approach. This involves writing continuously without worrying about grammar or structure. By doing this first thing in the morning, you can uncover subconscious thoughts and feelings that you might not have been aware of. It's a method of self-discovery that can lead to profound insights and a deeper understanding of your own psyche.

Another powerful journaling technique is to set specific prompts. These could be as simple as 'What am I grateful for today?' or as deep as 'What are my current fears?' By answering these prompts, you not only acknowledge various aspects of your life but also take steps toward addressing them. This routine can help foster a sense of gratitude, provide clarity on pressing issues, and ground you for the day ahead.

Consistency is key when it comes to journaling. Just like exercise, the benefits of journaling compound over time. The more you do it, the more you'll notice its positive impact on your mental clarity and emotional wellbeing. However, it's crucial to approach this practice without rigidity. If you miss a day, it's not the end of the world. What matters is getting back into the habit and making it a regular part of your morning routine.

Many ambitious professionals find that journaling helps them outline their goals and track progress. Writing down your short-term and long-term goals each morning can serve as a regular reminder of what you're working towards. This practice keeps your objectives at the forefront of your mind, motivating you throughout the day to take concrete steps toward achieving them.

Let's not forget the emotional aspect of journaling. Sometimes, the sheer act of writing down your feelings can alleviate emotional burdens. It's a safe space where you can vent without judgment. Whether you're facing stress from work, personal life, or simply the ups and downs of daily living, journaling serves as a therapeutic release that can significantly improve your emotional health.

For those who prefer more structure, bullet journaling can be an effective method. This system allows you to segment your thoughts, tasks, and reflections into manageable chunks. Often, it includes lists, daily logs, and even diagrams. The visual and organized nature of bullet journaling can make it easier to track progress and identify patterns in your thoughts and behaviors.

Moreover, journaling is a space to record milestones and achievements. Acknowledging these successes, no matter how small, can boost your self-esteem and reinforce a positive mindset. When you periodically review your journal entries, you'll be able to see how much progress you've made, which can be incredibly motivating. This practice not only enhances your emotional wellbeing but also promotes sustained personal growth.

Another key benefit of journaling is its ability to clarify decision-making processes. When faced with a tough decision, writing down the pros and cons can help you weigh your options more objectively. This form of self-dialogue often leads to clearer insights and more confident choices, minimizing the mental clutter that comes with indecision.

Additionally, morning journaling enhances self-discipline. By committing to this practice, you demonstrate to yourself that you value your mental and emotional health. Over time, this consistent act of self-care can translate into other areas of your life. You may find that you're more disciplined in your professional tasks, relationships, and other personal habits.

For those who are new to journaling, starting can be the hardest part. If you find yourself staring at a blank page, try starting with a simple question: 'How am I feeling today?' This question can act as a springboard, encouraging you to explore your thoughts and emotions further. Once you get started, you might be surprised at how naturally your thoughts begin to flow onto the page.

In essence, journaling is both a mirror and a window. It's a mirror that reflects your innermost thoughts and feelings, providing clarity on who you are and where you stand. At the same time, it's a window that offers a glimpse into your future aspirations and goals. By regularly looking into this mirror and peering through this window, you equip yourself with the clarity and motivation needed to tackle each day with purpose.

Remember, journaling is a personal practice. There is no right or wrong way to do it. Whether you prefer writing long paragraphs or bullet points, whether you use a digital app or a physical notebook, the key is to find a method that resonates with you. The most important thing is that you're taking time each morning to connect with yourself, set intentions, and foster mental and emotional clarity.

Mental and emotional wellbeing isn't a destination but a journey. By making journaling a part of your daily routine, you give yourself the tools to navigate this journey with greater clarity and purpose. So, grab your pen, find a quiet spot, and start writing. Your path to clarity begins with a single sentence.

Chapter 8: Planning and Setting Intentions

A powerful morning routine starts with a well-thought-out plan and clear intentions. By dedicating time each evening to outline your top priorities for the next day, you eliminate the morning scramble and set a purposeful tone. Incorporating affirmations into this routine can amplify your sense of direction and commitment, driving you toward your goals with unwavering focus. The act of planning doesn't just organize your tasks; it consciously aligns your actions with your broader life objectives. So, take a few moments to chart your day, visualize your successes, and speak your intentions out loud. This foundational practice fosters a sense of achievement and cultivates an empowered mindset ready to tackle the day's challenges head-on.

Daily Planning Techniques

To truly harness the power of a well-structured morning routine, it's essential to incorporate effective daily planning techniques. Planning out your day right from the start can be a game-changer, setting the tone for a productive and focused journey ahead. You're not merely reacting to whatever comes your way; you're proactively dictating the flow of your day.

Let's start with the basics: setting priorities. Begin by identifying the most critical tasks you need to accomplish. Prioritizing isn't just about listing what needs to be done; it's about strategically organizing tasks so that the most crucial ones are addressed first. It's often said that if you have to eat a frog, eat it first thing in the morning. In other words, tackle your hardest task right

CHAPTER 8: PLANNING AND SETTING INTENTIONS

away—it gives you a sense of achievement early on.

Next, consider the art of time blocking. This technique involves segmenting your day into blocks of time dedicated to specific tasks or activities. By doing this, you avoid the pitfalls of multitasking and can immerse yourself fully in each endeavor. For instance, you could allocate one hour in the morning solely for deep work—those tasks requiring intense focus with minimal distractions—and reserve the afternoon for meetings or creative brainstorming sessions.

Another powerful tool is the use of a daily planner or a digital task management system. Planners come in various formats—some people prefer traditional paper planners for the tactile experience, while others might opt for digital versions that sync across devices. What matters most is consistency in using these tools. Jot down your tasks, deadlines, and even minor details. This process not only clears your mind but also serves as a visual cue, steering you back on track if you veer off course.

Reflect for a moment on the value of flexibility. Rigid schedules can sometimes cause more stress than they alleviate. While it's vital to have a plan, it's equally important to allow room for adjustments. Unexpected challenges and opportunities can arise, and being adaptable ensures you can pivot without feeling overwhelmed.

Equally important is the habit of reviewing your day. Spend a few minutes at the end of each workday evaluating what you accomplished and where you could improve. This reflection helps fine-tune your planning skills over time. Did you underestimate the time required for certain tasks? Were there avoidable distractions? Use these insights to adjust your approach for the next day.

Consider integrating the "Two-Minute Rule" into your planning. Based on the concept that if a task takes less than two minutes, do it immediately, this rule helps to prevent small tasks from becoming larger, more daunting chores. Clearing out these minor tasks can create a surprisingly significant amount of mental space, enabling you to focus on more substantial work.

Now, let's talk about leveraging the power of routine in your planning. A consistent morning routine provides a sense of structure and predictability, which is crucial for staying organized. Perhaps you might find value in creating a morning checklist. This could include everything from making your bed to preparing your breakfast, exercising, and of course, your initial planning session for the day.

Technology can be both a boon and a bane in daily planning. Utilize productivity apps that offer features like task prioritization, calendar integration, and even reminders for regular breaks. However, be wary of overloading your system with too many tools. Find a few that work for you and stick with them—sometimes, simplicity is the ultimate sophistication.

While planning for professional tasks, don't neglect personal goals and self-care. Incorporate activities that promote your overall well-being, such as exercise, meditation, or even a hobby that you love. A balanced plan ensures that you don't burn out and helps maintain a high level of productivity over the long term.

The Five-Minute Journal is another excellent strategy for daily planning. This technique was made popular by productivity experts and involves spending five minutes jotting down what you are grateful for and what you hope to accomplish. By incorporating gratitude, you shift your mindset to focus on the positive aspects of your day, which can increase motivation and reduce stress.

As we dig deeper, let's reconsider the role of deadlines. Setting realistic but firm deadlines can create a sense of urgency and prevent procrastination. Even if there's no external pressure to complete a task by a specific time, self-imposed deadlines can keep you accountable.

Breaking down larger projects into bite-sized tasks can also dramatically enhance your daily planning. Large goals can often seem overwhelming, but dividing them into smaller, more manageable tasks makes them less daunting and easier to accomplish.

Incorporating "themed days" can further refine your planning strategies. This concept involves dedicating specific days of the week to different types of tasks. For example, you might reserve Mondays for meetings, Wednesdays for creative work, and Fridays for administrative tasks. Themed days can reduce context switching, allowing deeper focus on each type of task.

Mind-mapping can be an invaluable technique for brainstorming and organizing your thoughts. Whether you use a mind-mapping software or just pen and paper, visually plotting out your tasks and ideas can provide clarity and reveal connections you might not see in list format.

Lastly, don't underestimate the power of starting your day with a clear mind. Simple mindfulness practices, like a five-minute breathing exercise, can center your thoughts and make your planning session more effective. Starting from a place of calm can make all the difference in how you execute your plans.

In summary, mastering daily planning involves a combination of setting clear priorities, time blocking, using effective tools, and embracing flexibility. By reviewing and reflecting on your progress, integrating small but impactful habits like the Two-Minute Rule, and regularly recalibrating your approach, you'll find that your productivity, focus, and well-being soar to new heights.

These daily planning techniques are invaluable as they align your actions with your intentions, driving you closer to your goals with each passing day. As you embark on or refine your journey, remember that the key to effective planning is consistency coupled with mindful adaptability.

The Role of Affirmations

In the journey of planning and setting intentions, affirmations play an instrumental role. They are not just positive statements we repeat; they are powerful tools that shape our reality and set the tone for our day. Affirmations help anchor our intentions and provide a roadmap for our thoughts and actions. When used effectively, they can transform our mindset, build resilience, and propel us towards our goals with unwavering confidence.

At the heart of affirmations lies a simple yet profound principle: the thoughts we cultivate influence our reality. Imagine starting your day with an affirmation like, "I am focused, energized, and ready to tackle any challenge that comes my way." Repeating this statement sets a precedent for how you'll face your tasks and interactions. It's like setting a mental alarm clock reminding you of your potential and purpose.

For ambitious professionals, affirmations can serve as a daily touchpoint for self-reflection and motivation. They are the inner dialogue that counters the inevitable doubts and fears we all face. By regularly integrating affirmations into your morning routine, you create a mental framework where positive, intentional thoughts can thrive. This practice cultivates an attitude of success, even in the face of adversity.

But how exactly do affirmations function in the context of planning and setting intentions? First, they help in crystallizing what you want to achieve. For instance, if one of your intentions is to enhance your productivity, your affirmation might be, "I manage my time efficiently and consistently meet my goals." This doesn't just state a desire; it declares a belief, transforming your intention into something tangible and actionable.

Affirmations also bridge the gap between planning and action. Crafting a to-do list or setting intentions for the day requires clarity and determination. By pairing these tasks with affirmations, you reinforce your commitment to them. As you plan out your morning, saying aloud or writing down affirmations can solidify your focus and keep you grounded in your objectives.

For example, imagine you have a big presentation at work. Planning your morning to include preparation for this presentation is essential. An accompanying affirmation like, "I am confident, well-prepared, and articulate," can help quell nerves and reinforce self-belief. This isn't just about repeating words; it's about aligning your mindset with your actions to create a harmonious pursuit of your goals.

One of the most significant benefits of affirmations is the way they can enhance our emotional and mental wellbeing. Life, especially for high-achieving professionals, can often be stressful and overwhelming. Affirmations serve as a mental checkpoint, allowing you to pause, reflect, and recalibrate. Phrases such as, "I am capable of handling whatever comes my way," can be incredibly grounding, offering a sense of control and stability amidst chaos.

Moreover, affirmations can be personalized to fit your unique needs and aspirations. Whether you're aiming to improve your focus, build confidence, or enhance your productivity, there's an affirmation for that. Creating a personalized list of affirmations that resonate with you makes them more effective. When these affirmations reflect your deepest intentions and desires, they become ingrained in your psyche, subtly influencing your decisions and actions.

It's important to note that affirmations are most powerful when used consistently. Like any other aspect of a morning routine, they thrive on repetition and regular practice. You wouldn't expect to develop a new skill after just one attempt, and the same applies to affirmations. Consistent reinforcement helps embed these positive statements into your subconscious mind, making them an integral part of your belief system.

Incorporating affirmations into your morning routine doesn't have to be complicated. It can be as simple as taking a few moments during your daily planning session to jot down a few positive statements. Or, if you prefer, you could start your day by looking in the mirror and repeating your affirmations out loud. The key is to find a method that feels authentic and manageable for you, ensuring it becomes a sustainable part of your routine.

Imagine waking up each morning with a clear sense of purpose and direction. Affirmations can help make this a reality. By setting positive intentions first thing in the morning, you set the stage for a productive and fulfilling day. They become a mental compass, guiding your thoughts, actions, and reactions throughout the day, helping you stay aligned with your goals and values.

Furthermore, affirmations can act as a buffer against negativity and self-doubt. In the high-stakes world of ambitious professionals, it's easy to get bogged down by criticism, setbacks, or the internal pressure to excel. Affirmations reinforce your confidence and belief in your abilities, providing a counter-narrative to any negative thoughts that might arise. They remind you of your strengths and potential, offering a source of encouragement and motivation.

The effectiveness of affirmations is also backed by scientific research. Studies in cognitive psychology have shown that positive self-affirmation practices can reduce stress, increase wellbeing, and improve performance. When we affirm our positive qualities and intentions, we create a mental environment that fosters growth, resilience, and success.

Incorporating affirmations into your planning and intention-setting process is a holistic approach that encompasses both your mental and emotional spheres. It's about aligning your inner dialogue with your external actions, creating a cohesive and empowered state of being. By doing so, you not only optimize your productivity but also enhance your overall sense of wellbeing and fulfillment.

Take a moment to reflect on your current morning routine. How often do you set intentions, and how consistently do you follow through with them? Now, imagine layering in affirmations that support those intentions. Picture yourself starting the day with a clear, positive statement that mirrors your goals and aspirations. Visualize the impact this practice could have on your productivity, mindset, and overall success.

As you integrate affirmations into your routine, remember to be patient and kind to yourself. Personal growth is a journey, not a destination. Consistent practice, coupled with genuine belief in your affirmations, will gradually yield significant results. The more you affirm your capabilities and intentions, the more you'll see these reflected in your daily life.

In conclusion, affirmations are a vital component of planning and setting intentions. They empower you to shape your reality, reinforce your goals, and navigate your day with confidence and clarity. By making affirmations a regular part of your morning routine, you're investing in a practice that nurtures both your personal and professional growth. Embrace the power of affirmations, and watch as they transform your mornings, your mindset, and your life.

Chapter 9: Personal Development

To elevate our lives and careers, personal development plays a pivotal role in a successful morning routine. This quest for self-improvement isn't just about productivity hacks or time management; it's about transforming ourselves into lifelong learners who continuously seek growth. Embracing new skills, diving into intriguing books, or indulging in the wisdom of audiobooks during your morning regimen can fuel your mind and spirit. By committing to a structured approach to personal development, you're not only enhancing your capability to handle daily tasks but also setting the foundation for a more enriched and fulfilling life. As you weave these elements into your mornings, you'll find that each day becomes a building block for both professional excellence and personal satisfaction.

Learning and Skill Building

Personal development is an ongoing journey, and one of the most effective ways to fuel this journey is through continuous learning and skill building. When we invest time in acquiring new knowledge and honing our skills, we give ourselves the tools to navigate life's complexities with more confidence and competence. This becomes even more impactful when integrated into our morning routines, setting a foundation for a productive and fulfilling day.

The morning is an opportune time for learning because our brains tend to be more alert and receptive after a good night's sleep. By dedicating time to personal growth activities in the morning, we ensure that they become a priority, rather than an afterthought squeezed into a busy day. The quiet and calm of the early hours can also provide the ideal environment for focused, uninterrupted learning.

There are various ways to incorporate learning into your morning routine. You might start with a simple daily habit like reading a few pages of a book, listening to an educational podcast, or watching a short, informative video. These activities can expand your knowledge base and introduce you to new ideas and perspectives. Over time, they can also improve your cognitive abilities, enhancing your overall brain health.

Moreover, the type of content you engage with in the morning can set the tone for the rest of your day. Inspirational books, for example, can motivate you to tackle your tasks with enthusiasm. On the other hand, reading up on industry trends can prepare you for important meetings or projects. The key is to choose content that aligns with your personal or professional goals, making your morning learning sessions both meaningful and enjoyable.

Some individuals might prefer more interactive forms of learning, such as online courses or webinars. Many platforms offer short, digestible lessons that can be easily integrated into a morning routine. These sessions can cover a wide range of topics—from mastering a new language to learning coding. Scheduling these activities in the morning ensures that you approach them with a fresh mind and are able to retain information more effectively.

Another approach to learning in the morning involves practicing new skills. Whether it's playing a musical instrument, practicing a new language, or dabbling in creative writing, dedicating time to skill practice can yield significant benefits. The repetition and consistency offered by daily practice help solidify new skills, turning them into second nature over time.

Consider the example of learning a new language. Spending even just 15 minutes every morning on vocabulary drills, grammar exercises, or conversational practice can accumulate to substantial progress over the weeks and months. Similarly, practicing a new instrument in the morning can be an invigorating and peaceful way to start the day.

Additionally, technology can offer a plethora of opportunities for learning and skill-building. There are countless apps designed for educational purposes, such as language learning apps, coding tutorials, and brain training games. These apps often come with features that allow you to set daily goals and track your progress, adding an element of accountability to your learning process.

For many ambitious professionals, staying ahead in their field requires continuous learning. Developing a habit of engaging with industry-specific content in the morning can keep you updated on the latest trends, technologies, and best practices. Subscribing to relevant newsletters, blogs, or journals and dedicating some morning time to reading these can provide insights that could be pivotal for your career growth.

Another important aspect of learning and skill building is reflection. Taking a moment each morning to reflect on what you learned the previous day can reinforce your knowledge and provide clarity on how to apply it in real-life situations. You might jot down key takeaways in a journal or discuss them with a mentor or colleague. This reflective practice not only enhances your learning but also encourages a growth mindset, fostering a continuous willingness to improve and adapt.

Networking with like-minded individuals and participating in learning communities can also amplify your personal development efforts. Engaging in online forums, attending meet-ups, or joining study groups can offer opportunities for collaborative learning. Sharing knowledge and experiences with others can deepen your understanding and introduce you to new perspectives that you might not have considered otherwise.

Ultimately, the goal is to make learning and skill building an integral part of your morning routine, creating a habit that consistently propels you towards your personal and professional aspirations. The benefits of this practice are multifaceted. Not only does it contribute to your intellectual growth, but it also provides a sense of accomplishment and purpose as you start your day. By committing to lifelong learning, you embrace the essence of personal development, continually evolving to reach your fullest potential.

Your journey of learning and skill building doesn't have to be daunting. Start with small, manageable steps that fit seamlessly into your morning routine. Over time, these small efforts can lead to substantial growth, turning each morning into a powerful catalyst for personal and professional development.

With this approach, you're not just preparing for your day—you're preparing for a lifetime of growth and success.

Reading and Audiobooks

Reading and listening to audiobooks can be transformative habits that significantly enhance personal development. Incorporating these activities into your morning routine can set a tone of continuous learning and intellectual growth. As you awaken your mind and prepare for the day's challenges, reading and audiobooks can provide inspiration, knowledge, and a sense of accomplishment. By dedicating time in the morning to consume valuable content, you create a foundation for lifelong learning and personal growth.

Let's explore why reading and audiobooks are such powerful tools for personal development. First and foremost, reading stimulates the brain and enhances cognitive functions. It's been shown to improve focus, concentration, and analytical thinking. By starting your day with a book, you're essentially giving your brain a warm-up exercise, much like stretching before a workout. This mental stimulation is crucial, especially in the morning when your mind is fresh and receptive.

Moreover, reading exposes you to new ideas, perspectives, and information that can broaden your horizons. Imagine starting your day with a few pages from a book on leadership or personal growth. The insights you gain can spark new ideas and provide you with strategies to tackle challenges more effectively. Over time, the knowledge you accumulate through reading will become a reservoir you can draw upon in both your personal and professional life.

On the other hand, audiobooks offer a unique advantage for busy individuals. They allow you to consume valuable content without requiring you to sit down with a physical book. This can be particularly beneficial during your morning commute or while engaging in other activities like exercising or preparing breakfast. Audiobooks can turn seemingly mundane tasks into opportunities for learning and self-improvement.

Another compelling reason to engage in reading and audiobooks in the morning is the positive effect they have on your mood and mindset. Inspirational books or chapters filled with motivational content can uplift your spirits and set a positive tone for the day. Additionally, narratives and stories can be incredibly engaging, providing an enjoyable way to transition from the slumber of night to the activities of the day.

To truly integrate reading and audiobooks into your morning routine, it's essential to be intentional about it. Designate a specific time and place for reading. It could be during breakfast, right after your morning exercise, or even while you're enjoying your first cup of coffee. Having a dedicated spot and time helps to make it a consistent habit.

Start with setting a realistic goal. You don't need to read an entire book in one sitting; a few pages each morning can make a significant impact over time. Gradually increase the amount of time you spend reading or listening to audiobooks as you become more comfortable with your routine. Consistency is key. Just like any other habit, the more you do it, the easier it becomes, and the greater the benefits you'll reap.

Choosing the right material is also critical. Select books and audiobooks that align with your personal and professional goals. Non-fiction books on self-development, business, and psychology can provide actionable insights. Fiction, on the other hand, can stimulate creativity and empathy. Having a balanced mix ensures that you're nurturing both your intellectual and emotional well-being.

Here are some practical tips to make the most of your reading and audiobook sessions:

1. **Curate a Reading List:** Identify books that resonate with your interests and goals. Having a list ensures that you always have a next book lined up, preventing unnecessary gaps between readings.
2. **Use Book Summaries:** For days when time is short, book summaries can provide the essence of a book's value in a fraction of the time. They're not a substitute for reading full books but can be a great supplement.
3. **Take Notes:** Jot down key takeaways, insights, and quotes. This reinforces what you've learned and serves as a quick reference for future

use.

4. **Set Milestones:** Break your reading into manageable chunks. Set milestones and celebrate small victories, such as finishing a chapter or reaching a particular section.
5. **Discuss What You Read:** Engage in discussions with peers or join book clubs. Talking about what you've learned deepens your understanding and provides fresh perspectives.

If you're new to audiobooks, consider starting with short, engaging titles. Many platforms offer free trials or samples, allowing you to explore different genres and narrators. Finding a narrator whose voice and style you enjoy can greatly enhance your audiobook experience.

The potential for transformative growth through reading and audiobooks is immense, yet it's worth noting that the key lies in integration and consistency. This isn't about sporadic, one-off bursts of reading but rather about weaving these activities seamlessly into your morning ritual.

As you develop this habit, pay attention to how it influences other areas of your life. You might find your communication skills improving, your ability to think critically and solve problems enhanced, and your overall stress levels reduced. Books have a way of imparting wisdom that transcends the written word, offering solace, motivation, and actionable advice that can make a tangible difference in your life.

Whether it's the profound insights from a self-improvement classic, the innovative strategies from a business book, or the deeply human experiences found in fiction, reading has a magical way of expanding your horizons and enriching your soul. And when it comes to audiobooks, the convenience and multifaceted nature of auditory learning can make this medium an invaluable part of your personal development arsenal.

Make a commitment to yourself to embrace the power of reading and audiobooks as part of your morning routine. Spend those first precious minutes or hours of the day immersing yourself in the thoughts and ideas of great thinkers, storytellers, and leaders. In doing so, you'll not only enhance your productivity and well-being but also set yourself on a path of continuous

CHAPTER 9: PERSONAL DEVELOPMENT

growth and lifelong learning.

Chapter 10: The Role of Sleep

Sleep isn't just a night-time ritual; it's the cornerstone of a highly productive day. Quality sleep has a profound impact on your mental clarity, emotional wellbeing, and overall productivity. Without adequate rest, even the most meticulously planned morning routine can fall apart. Prioritizing sleep allows you to wake up refreshed, energetic, and ready to tackle your goals. Remember, it's not just about the quantity of sleep but the quality. Incorporating good sleep hygiene practices—like maintaining a consistent sleep schedule, creating a restful environment, and minimizing blue light exposure before bed—can significantly enhance the restorative power of your sleep. So, as you look to unlock your full potential each morning, never underestimate the crucial role that sleep plays in setting you up for success.

Importance of Quality Sleep

Sleep, often overlooked in the quest for productivity and personal growth, plays a foundational role that can't be ignored. The rejuvenating power of quality sleep affects not just your mornings but ripples through your entire day. For ambitious professionals aiming to maximize their productivity, understanding the value of quality sleep is indispensable.

Consider the moments when you've woken up from a restful night's sleep. Your mind is clearer, your mood lighter, and your ability to focus is markedly enhanced. Quality sleep is directly correlated with cognitive function, emotional wellbeing, and physical health. It's the unseen cornerstone of a successful morning routine.

Professionals often face demanding schedules, with responsibilities pulling them in countless directions. Amid this chaos, sleep can easily become a casualty. However, rather than thinking of sleep as a passive act, it should be viewed as an active investment in your future performance and clarity.

To understand the importance of quality sleep, let's first delve into its effects on cognitive functions. During deep sleep, the brain processes and consolidates information from the day. This phase, often referred to as slow-wave sleep, plays a vital role in memory formation and learning. Without adequate deep sleep, your ability to grasp new concepts and retain information is significantly compromised.

In addition to cognitive benefits, quality sleep also promotes emotional regulation. Have you ever noticed how everything seems more manageable after a full night's rest? That's no coincidence. Sleep helps regulate the hormones that control mood, aiding in stress reduction and emotional stability. For someone navigating the challenges of a high-stakes work environment, steady emotional control is a tremendous asset.

Another critical aspect is the impact of sleep on physical health. While you sleep, your body undergoes essential repair processes. Cells are repaired, muscles grow, and tissues are regenerated. This not only ensures that you wake up feeling physically restored but also builds resilience against illnesses. For anyone looking to maintain peak physical condition for their demanding lifestyle, quality sleep is non-negotiable.

Furthermore, sleep influences metabolic functions. Inadequate sleep disrupts the balance of hunger-regulating hormones like ghrelin and leptin, often leading to poor dietary choices and weight gain. By prioritizing sleep, you indirectly support better nutrition and hydration choices, both of which are fundamental to sustaining energy levels throughout the day.

Imagine trying to craft the perfect morning routine while constantly battling the fog of sleep deprivation. It's a scenario doomed for failure. Without quality sleep as the underpinning, even the most meticulously planned morning routines will falter. Productivity hacks, advanced scheduling, and motivational techniques lose their effectiveness against the tide of exhaustion.

As we dive deeper into the role of sleep, it becomes apparent that sleep isn't merely a period of rest but an active phase essential for rebooting both the brain and body. When treated with the importance it deserves, you create a virtuous cycle: better sleep leads to more productive mornings, which in turn lead to more successful and fulfilling days.

The modern professional landscape often glorifies the 'hustle' culture, where long hours are mistaken for productivity. However, this can be detrimental if it results in sleep deprivation. Learning to manage your work-life balance in a way that prioritizes sleep will pay dividends in sustained productivity and wellbeing.

Sleep isn't just a break from the hustle; it's where the magic happens. Your body and mind accomplish extraordinary feats during sleep, preparing you to tackle challenges with vigor and creativity. Entrepreneurs and high-achievers must shift from viewing sleep as optional to considering it a fundamental component of their success strategy.

When you recognize that quality sleep affects every facet of your life—from decision-making abilities to long-term health—you can start to see why it must be the cornerstone of any effective morning routine. Making sleep a priority will impact your ability to wake up early, enhance your mental clarity, and focus on tasks that align with your goals.

So, how do you ensure that you're getting quality sleep? It begins with understanding sleep hygiene—cultivating habits that improve your sleep environment and practice. Consistency is key. Going to bed and waking up at the same time each day can establish a stable sleep-wake cycle, making it easier to attain restorative sleep.

Creating a sleep-conducive environment also plays a significant role. Keep your bedroom cool, dark, and quiet to encourage uninterrupted slumber. Investing in a comfortable mattress and pillows can also make a substantial difference. Remember, your bedroom should be a sanctuary for rest, not a secondary office.

Avoid consuming caffeine or engaging in stimulating activities close to bedtime. Instead, develop a calming pre-sleep routine. Rituals like reading, listening to soft music, or meditating can signal your body that it's time to wind down and prepare for sleep.

Equally important is limiting screen time before bed. The blue light emitted by phones, tablets, and computers can interfere with the production of melatonin, the hormone regulating sleep. Consider setting a 'digital curfew' to disconnect from electronic devices at least an hour before bedtime.

An often underappreciated component of quality sleep is the role of mental clarity and reduced stress. Engaging in relaxation techniques such as deep breathing exercises or progressive muscle relaxation can alleviate anxiety, a common culprit for restless nights. Pairing these practices with gratitude journaling can also shift focus from stressors to positive aspects of your day, creating a peaceful mindset conducive to restful sleep.

Additionally, being mindful of your body's rhythms and aligning your sleep schedule with your natural circadian clock is crucial. Morning people, or 'larks', may find it easier to maintain a routine that aligns with early waking times, whereas 'night owls' might need to gradually adjust their habits to ensure they attain the benefits of waking up early without sacrificing sleep quality.

At the end of the day, embracing the importance of quality sleep is about fostering a lifestyle that harmonizes with your goals. This doesn't mean you need to overhaul your life overnight. Start small. Incremental changes in sleep habits can lead to significant improvements. Once you experience the enhanced productivity and wellbeing that comes from quality sleep, you'll find it easier to prioritize and defend your sleep from the many demands of modern life.

Quality sleep is the secret weapon in the arsenal of ambitious professionals. It fuels creativity, sustains energy, and fortifies the body and mind against the rigors of daily challenges. When you embed quality sleep into your ethos, you set the stage for a life of sustained productivity, health, and personal growth. It all starts with recognizing that the path to a successful morning—and, indeed, a successful life—begins with the embrace of quality sleep.

Sleep Hygiene Tips

Sleep, often overlooked in our relentless pursuit of success, is a cornerstone of productivity and wellbeing. Quality sleep sets the stage for all that follows, including the cornerstone elements of your morning routine. It transforms how you handle tasks, respond to challenges, and sustain energy levels throughout the day. Let's look into some effective sleep hygiene tips that can help you create an optimal environment for restorative sleep and, by extension, a productive morning.

Firstly, maintaining a consistent sleep schedule is paramount. Going to bed and waking up at the same time every day—even on weekends—can significantly improve the quality of your sleep. Our bodies thrive on routine, and a regular sleep-wake cycle anchors our circadian rhythms. When these rhythms are disrupted, we experience reduced sleep quality and increased fatigue. Consistency helps train your body's internal clock and can make falling asleep and waking up easier.

Equally important is creating a bedroom environment that promotes sleep. Consider your bedroom as your sleep sanctuary. Dark, quiet, and cool environments are the most conducive to quality sleep. Use blackout curtains, minimize noise with earplugs or white noise machines, and keep the room temperature between 60-67°F. If light pollution is an issue, an eye mask can work wonders in masking any intrusive light.

The role of your bed itself shouldn't be underestimated. A comfortable mattress and supportive pillows are crucial for good sleep. Everyone's preferences are different, so take the time to find what works best for you. Additionally, keep your bed reserved for sleep and intimacy. Using it for work, watching TV, or browsing social media sends mixed signals to your brain and can make it harder to associate your bed with restful sleep.

Speaking of technology, the blue light emitted by phones, tablets, and computers can interfere with the production of melatonin, the hormone responsible for regulating sleep. It's advisable to limit screen time at least an hour before bed. If that's not possible, consider using blue light filters available on most devices or purchasing blue light blocking glasses.

CHAPTER 10: THE ROLE OF SLEEP

Another often overlooked aspect of sleep hygiene is your pre-sleep routine. Just as a morning routine sets the tone for your day, an evening routine signals your body that it's time to wind down. Engaging in calming activities like reading, meditating, or taking a warm bath can help transition you into a state suitable for sleep. Exercise can also impact your sleep quality. While regular physical activity is essential for overall health, try to avoid vigorous workouts late in the evening as they can be too stimulating.

Caffeine and alcohol consumption are other factors that can significantly impact sleep quality. Caffeine is a potent stimulant, so try to limit your intake to the morning hours. Even if you don't feel jittery, caffeine can sneak into your system and disrupt your sleep. Alcohol, on the other hand, might make you feel drowsy initially but can lead to poor sleep quality and frequent awakenings throughout the night.

Nutrition plays a more crucial role than you might realize. Eating large meals or spicy foods close to bedtime can cause discomfort and disrupt your sleep. Instead, opt for a light, balanced snack if you find yourself hungry before bed. Foods rich in magnesium, such as nuts or leafy greens, can help relax muscles and contribute to better sleep. Additionally, staying hydrated is essential, but try to limit fluid intake in the evening to minimize nighttime awakenings.

Your mental state before bedtime is also worth considering. Stress and anxiety are significant barriers to restful sleep. Techniques such as progressive muscle relaxation, deep breathing exercises, and mindfulness meditation can help calm your mind. Journaling before bed is another effective tactic; by writing down your thoughts, you can clear your mind and spare yourself the worry loop that often keeps people awake.

If you're still having trouble falling asleep despite implementing these tips, don't hesitate to consult a healthcare professional. Sleep disorders like insomnia, sleep apnea, or restless leg syndrome might require more specialized interventions. There's no shame in seeking help—improving your sleep health can have profoundly positive impacts on your overall quality of life.

Remember, sleep is not a luxury; it's a necessity. Implementing good sleep hygiene practices can make an enormous difference in the quality of your sleep and your waking hours. By investing time and effort into perfecting your sleep routine, you lay down a solid foundation for a successful and productive morning routine, unlocking your full potential as an ambitious professional.

Chapter 11: Case Studies and Success Stories

Imagine being able to peek into the morning routines of some of the most successful people in the world and everyday individuals who've turned their mornings into a catalyst for productivity and personal growth. This chapter embodies just that spirit. We'll dive into an array of real-life examples, from celebrated figures like CEOs and athletes to unsung heroes who've mastered their mornings to achieve astounding results. These stories showcase diverse strategies, illustrating that there's no one-size-fits-all solution, but rather a toolkit of practices that can be adapted to fit your needs. By studying these transformative routines and testimonials, you'll gain invaluable insights and draw inspiration to craft a morning ritual that sets the tone for a thriving day ahead.

Famous Figures and Their Routines

When diving into the morning routines of successful individuals, it's hard not to marvel at the varied yet intentional ways they kickstart their days. These famous figures, whether from the world of business, art, or science, have mastered the art of the morning routine to amplify their productivity and wellbeing. By examining some of these routines, we can gain insights and inspiration for creating our own powerful starts to the day.

One highly-discussed figure is Steve Jobs. The co-founder of Apple was known for his singular focus and minimalist lifestyle, traits that were reflected in his morning routine. Every morning, Jobs would ask himself, "If today were the last day of my life, would I want to do what I am about to do today?" This question kept him grounded and focused on his true priorities. He also maintained simple habits like eating a light breakfast and wearing virtually the same outfit every day, which minimized decision fatigue and allowed him to channel his energy towards more significant tasks.

On the opposite end of the spectrum was Winston Churchill, whose morning routine was surprisingly leisurely but no less effective. Churchill would wake up around 7:30 AM and spend the next few hours in bed, reading, writing letters, and catching up on the news. He would then have a hearty breakfast and begin his day of work around 11 AM. Churchill's routine underscores the importance of customizing your morning to fit your personal style and needs. For him, a slow start provided the mental clarity needed to lead a country through turbulent times.

Another notable example is Oprah Winfrey, whose morning practice revolves around self-care and mindfulness. Winfrey starts her day with a period of meditation, followed by exercise, typically a series of stretching routines and a run. After that, she spends some time journaling, which she calls her "gratitude exercise." By focusing on what she is grateful for, Winfrey primes her mind for positivity and success throughout the day. Breakfast usually follows, consisting of something wholesome and balanced like fruit, oatmeal, or eggs.

Benjamin Franklin's morning routine is a classic example that has inspired many. Franklin asked himself each morning, "What good shall I do this day?" This question set the tone for a day focused on productivity and moral fortitude. He would spend a considerable amount of time planning his day, outlining specific goals, and allotting time for work, meals, and personal development. His disciplined approach to mornings helped him achieve considerable success across multiple fields, including science, politics, and literature.

A modern-day success story that's often examined is that of Tim Ferriss, an entrepreneur and author known for his "life hacking" techniques. Ferriss advocates for a morning routine that includes a fixed sequence of activities designed to foster well-being and productivity. His mornings typically start with making his bed—a simple task that provides an immediate sense of accomplishment—followed by meditation, exercise, and consuming a high-protein breakfast. Ferriss also integrates journaling into his routine, using it as a tool for clearing his mind and setting his intentions for the day.

In the realm of creative arts, Maya Angelou's morning routine offers another fascinating perspective. Angelou preferred to leave her home early in the morning and head to a bare hotel room to write. She created a distraction-free environment that enabled her to focus purely on her creativity. Her routine underscores the importance of finding a personal space that fosters productivity, an essential factor for anyone aiming to maximize their morning potential.

Elon Musk, the CEO of SpaceX and Tesla, is yet another example of someone who uses his mornings to his advantage. Musk wakes up around 7 AM, skipping breakfast to immediately dive into a rigorous schedule of critical tasks and meetings. He prioritizes time for problem-solving and strategic planning, often working on the highest-priority projects first. Despite his hectic schedule, Musk incorporates brief moments of exercise to maintain his energy levels. His approach illustrates how a well-planned morning can handle immense professional demands.

From the literary world, we have the routines of Haruki Murakami, a Japanese author known for his discipline and dedication. Murakami wakes up at 4 AM every day, writing for five to six hours before heading out for a run or swim. He believes that maintaining a routine is crucial for creativity and productivity. By incorporating both mental and physical activities in his mornings, Murakami ensures that he is at his peak performance for the rest of the day.

Michelle Obama, the former First Lady of the United States, also emphasizes the importance of incorporating physical exercise into her mornings. She is known to start her day with a workout that includes cardio and strength training. Obama's routine is a testament to the idea that physical well-being is inseparable from mental and emotional health. By making exercise a priority, she sets a tone of discipline and focus for the rest of her activities.

Even historical figures like Mahatma Gandhi had morning routines that contributed to their effectiveness. Gandhi's mornings were marked by prayer, spinning thread, and a light, simple breakfast. The act of spinning was not just a chore for him but a meditative practice that aligned with his principles of simplicity and self-sufficiency. Gandhi's morning routine demonstrates that even simple, repetitive tasks can have profound impacts when they are imbued with meaning and purpose.

Anna Wintour, the influential editor-in-chief of Vogue, starts her mornings with a game of tennis. This vigorous activity not only keeps her fit but also mentally sharp, ready to tackle the challenges of running one of the most significant fashion magazines in the world. Wintour's choice of a physically demanding sport highlights the fact that high-energy activities can also serve as a source of motivation and strength for the day ahead.

The routines of these famous figures, though varied, share a common thread: intentionality. Each of these individuals has designed a morning routine that caters to their specific needs, goals, and lifestyle. They have found ways to incorporate activities that bring clarity, energy, and focus into their mornings, setting the stage for a productive and fulfilling day.

By examining these routines, we can draw lessons and adapt elements to fit our own lives. Whether it's asking a reflective question like Steve Jobs, slowing down the morning pace like Winston Churchill, or integrating physical activity like Michelle Obama, the key lies in understanding what invigorates and prepares us for the day. These successful individuals show that a well-crafted morning routine is not just a series of tasks but a powerful tool for fostering long-term productivity and wellbeing.

So take a moment to reflect on these routines and think about how you can tailor your own morning to set yourself up for success. Uncovering the morning rituals of these iconic figures provides not just a blueprint but also a wellspring of inspiration to craft a routine that resonates with your aspirations and daily demands.

CHAPTER 11: CASE STUDIES AND SUCCESS STORIES

Real-Life Testimonials

In the quest for a perfect morning routine that fosters productivity and personal growth, nothing is more compelling than hearing from real people who have walked the path. Their stories resonate deeply because they are testaments to the transformative power of consistency, intentionality, and sometimes even a bit of trial and error. These real-life testimonials offer a glimpse into the diverse ways individuals have adapted morning routines to fit their unique lifestyles and goals.

Meet Jenna, a young professional working in a bustling city. Jenna's struggle was rooted in the overwhelming demands of her job coupled with a perpetually chaotic morning. She was constantly running late, stressed, and found it difficult to focus. Inspired by the concept of a morning routine, Jenna began experimenting with her mornings. Starting small, she set her alarm 30 minutes earlier and dedicated that time to stretching and a short meditation.

This seemingly minor change had a profound impact on her. Jenna shares, "I went from dreading mornings to actually looking forward to them. That quiet time for myself became sacred. I noticed I was more focused and less anxious throughout the day." Jenna's success didn't come overnight; it was through trial, adjusting her routine, and sticking with what worked that she finally found her flow.

Then there's Martin, a senior executive who had always believed that his productivity peaked late at night. However, he constantly felt groggy in the mornings and relied heavily on caffeine to jumpstart his day. Curious about the impact of an early rise, Martin committed to a four-week experiment. He didn't only change his sleep schedule; he also incorporated light exercise, hydration, and reading into his mornings.

The results were staggering. "I became a morning person," Martin observed with a chuckle. "I couldn't believe how much more I got done before even stepping into the office. It was like unlocking a more efficient version of myself." Martin's testimonial highlights the unexpected benefits of a well-structured morning, proving that even night owls can find value in adjusting their routines.

An even more transformative story is that of Lucy, a single mom balancing work, raising her children, and personal time. Her mornings used to be a blur of chaos, trying to get her kids ready for school while preparing for her own day. Lucy decided to reclaim her mornings by waking up before her children, using that uninterrupted time to plan her day and engage in quick, high-energy workouts.

Lucy shares, "I found that by investing that hour in myself, I was more patient and present for my kids. They noticed the difference too; mornings became less stressful for all of us." Her experience sheds light on how a structured morning routine can ripple out, positively impacting family dynamics and overall day-to-day harmony.

Finally, let's not overlook the newest generation of workers—remote employees like Ethan. Working from home blurred the lines between work and personal time, causing Ethan to struggle with burnout and lack of structure. He found solace in developing a morning routine that acted as a clear divider between his personal time and professional responsibilities.

"I started by adding simple things like making my bed and having a healthy breakfast," Ethan recounts. "Then I included journaling and a walk around the block. It's those small acts that set the tone for my day." Ethan's testimonial demonstrates that even minor adjustments can lead to significant improvements in one's mental and emotional wellbeing, especially in a work-from-home setting.

These real-life testimonials not only showcase the diverse ways people have adapted their morning routines but also serve as powerful motivators for those looking to make a change. Whether you're struggling with time management, battling anxiety, or simply looking to boost your productivity, these stories offer a beacon of hope. The key takeaway? Start small, be consistent, and tailor your routine to suit your needs.

Through the experiences of Jenna, Martin, Lucy, and Ethan, it becomes evident that morning routines are not one-size-fits-all. They are dynamic, evolving, and deeply personal. Their stories encourage us to be patient with ourselves, to try new things, and to stick with what works. The journey towards a more productive and fulfilling life starts with your mornings. Take

CHAPTER 11: CASE STUDIES AND SUCCESS STORIES

the first step, and who knows—you might just become the next success story.

Chapter 12: Tracking Your Progress

Tracking your progress is essential to creating a morning routine that sticks and truly enhances your life. Keeping a dedicated morning routine journal allows you to monitor what works and what needs adjustment, providing a clear record of your personal journey and growth. By regularly measuring the impact on your productivity, you can fine-tune your routine to align it perfectly with your goals. This practice transforms abstract goals into tangible achievements, offering a motivational boost as you see your milestones add up. Beyond productivity, tracking how you feel—physically, mentally, and emotionally—illuminates the complete picture of your well-being. It's all about celebrating small victories and recognizing patterns that help or hinder your progress, ultimately leading you toward a consistently fulfilling start to each day.

Keeping a Morning Routine Journal

One of the most effective ways to track your progress and ensure you're sticking to your morning routine is by keeping a journal. A morning routine journal is not just a log of your activities; it's a powerful instrument for self-reflection, growth, and accountability. By diligently recording your actions, thoughts, and feelings every morning, you build a tangible record of your journey, allowing you to celebrate your wins and learn from your setbacks.

Start small. Your journal doesn't have to be an elaborate affair filled with lengthy prose. A few bullet points, quick notes, or even a straightforward checklist will do the trick. The essential part is the consistency and the honesty with which you document your routine. Remember, this journal is for you. It's your private space to be completely candid about what's working and what's not.

Begin each entry with the basics: the date and the time you woke up. These initial details are crucial for identifying patterns, such as whether waking up at a consistent time impacts your productivity levels throughout the day. Did you wake up at your planned time, or did you hit the snooze button? Reflect on how you felt upon waking. Were you energized, groggy, motivated, or indifferent?

Make it a habit to jot down the core components of your morning routine. If your routine includes meditation, exercise, a healthy breakfast, and reading, note whether you completed each activity. Be specific. Instead of writing "Did my workout," you might note "30-minute yoga session focused on flexibility" or "Jogged 2 miles." This level of detail will help you see exactly which activities contribute most to your sense of accomplishment and well-being.

Remember, a morning routine journal is not just about what you did, but also how you experienced it. Reflect on your mood, energy levels, and any significant thoughts or insights. Did meditation bring you a sense of peace? Did stretching alleviate your back pain? Were you more focused and productive after reading a chapter of an inspiring book? These insights can be goldmines for refining your routine to better serve your needs.

Including a section for gratitude can also be transformative. When you take a moment each morning to write down a few things you're grateful for, you set a positive tone for the day ahead. This practice can enhance your overall outlook on life, reduce stress, and improve your mental health.

Over time, your journal will become a comprehensive map of your progress. You'll see patterns emerge, revealing which habits make the biggest positive impact on your day and which might need tweaking or replacing. You'll also gain valuable insights into how external factors—like sleep quality, diet, and stress levels—affect your performance and mood.

Let's not forget about the hurdles. It's crucial to document the challenges and obstacles you encounter. Maybe you had a late night and couldn't wake up early, or perhaps you didn't feel motivated to exercise. Note these struggles candidly. This isn't about beating yourself up; it's about understanding where you might need to make adjustments. Reflect on how you overcame these challenges, or if you didn't, what you might do differently next time.

As you fill your journal, occasionally flip back to previous entries. Observe your growth. Celebrate your milestones, no matter how small. Did you wake up early every day for a week? Fantastic! Did you meditate consistently despite a busy schedule? Applaud yourself. These reflections build confidence and motivation, reinforcing that you are capable of maintaining a productive morning routine.

Your morning routine journal can also act as a creative brainstorming space. If you find a particular routine isn't resonating with you, sketch out ideas for new activities to try. Perhaps a different type of exercise, a new meditation app, or incorporating music into your morning could make a difference.

Leverage technology if it suits you. Digital journals or apps designed for habit tracking can be incredibly useful. They often come with reminders, analytics, and the ability to share progress with an accountability partner or community, adding another layer of commitment.

For those who prefer traditional journaling, there's something uniquely powerful about putting pen to paper. The physical act of writing can make your reflections more concrete and memorable. Choose a notebook that feels right for you—something you'll look forward to using each morning. It could be a handmade leather-bound journal, a sleek minimalist planner, or even a simple spiral notebook. The key is to make it a pleasure, not a chore.

Finally, be patient with yourself. Developing a fulfilling morning routine and the habit of journaling takes time. There will be days when you fall off track, and that's perfectly okay. The journal is there to guide you back, to remind you of your goals, and to encourage you with evidence of your progress.

In summary, keeping a morning routine journal is an invaluable practice for anyone aiming to boost their productivity and personal growth. It provides a structured way to track your activities, reflect on your experiences, and make informed adjustments to your routine. Through consistent journaling, you'll build a rich tapestry of insights, celebrating your achievements and learning from your challenges. Embrace this practice, and watch how it transforms not just your mornings, but your entire day—and ultimately, your life.

Measuring Impact on Productivity

To truly understand the effectiveness of your morning routine, you must measure its impact on your productivity. This might sound like a daunting task, but with a systematic approach, you can gather valuable insights that will inform and inspire further improvements. It's not just about feeling good in the morning but seeing tangible progress in your daily life.

The first step in measuring impact is to establish a baseline. Start by documenting your current productivity levels before you introduce any changes to your morning routine. This could be as simple as rating your productivity on a scale from 1 to 10 at the end of each day. Note how much work you completed, your energy levels, and overall satisfaction with your performance. This baseline will serve as a reference point to measure growth and changes once you implement your new morning habits.

Next, clearly define what productivity means to you. For some, it might mean completing a specific number of tasks, while for others, it could involve levels of creativity or problem-solving abilities. Be specific about your goals, so the measures you track are aligned with what you consider productive. This step ensures that the data you gather is both relevant and meaningful.

Once a baseline is established and productivity is defined, introduce your new morning routine and begin tracking. Use a journal or digital tool to record your routine's components and their impact. Log details like what time you wake up, your activities, and how these correlate with your productivity throughout the day. For example, note whether a 10-minute meditation session improves your focus or if exercise boosts your energy levels.

In addition to subjective self-assessments, consider monitoring objective metrics. Track how much time you spend on key tasks, your progress on project milestones, and even how often you take breaks. Tools like time-tracking apps can provide a detailed view of where your time goes, helping you identify patterns and areas for improvement.

A critical part of the process is regular review. Set aside time each week to reflect on the data you've gathered. Are there consistent patterns? Do certain activities consistently enhance your productivity, while others seem less effective? Use this review to make informed adjustments. Remember, the goal isn't perfection; it's continuous improvement. For instance, if you find that journaling doesn't significantly impact your productivity, you might replace it with another activity like goal setting or strategic planning.

Feedback from peers and mentors can also provide valuable perspectives. Discuss your morning routine and productivity observations with trusted colleagues or mentors. They might offer insights or suggestions that you haven't considered, adding another layer to your self-assessment.

Keep in mind that measuring productivity is not just about quantity but also quality. High productivity doesn't mean working longer hours or completing more tasks but performing meaningful work that aligns with your goals. Reflect on the quality of your accomplishments and whether your morning routine helps you achieve a balanced, satisfying day.

Moreover, be open to the fact that measuring impact is an evolving process. What works today might not be as effective tomorrow due to changes in your personal or professional life. Seasonal shifts, new responsibilities, or even your evolving goals can influence how productive you feel. Staying adaptable and updating your routine accordingly is key to sustaining long-term productivity benefits.

It's also crucial to acknowledge and celebrate small wins. Recognizing even minor improvements can be incredibly motivating and serve as a testament to the effort you're putting into your morning routine. This positive reinforcement helps build momentum and encourages continued commitment to the routine you've crafted.

Sometimes, unexpected changes or disruptions will test the robustness of your morning routine. These moments offer a unique opportunity to evaluate the resilience of your habits. Were you able to adjust and still maintain your productivity levels, or did disruptions significantly impact your day? Analyzing these situations helps refine your routine to be more flexible and resilient in the face of change.

Lastly, always keep the bigger picture in mind. While daily and weekly measures are important, long-term impact is what you'll ultimately want to focus on. Periodically review your progress over months and even years. Are you advancing toward your broader career and personal goals? Has your overall wellbeing improved? The cumulative effect of a well-designed morning routine over time can be profound, offering not just greater productivity but a more fulfilling life.

In summary, measuring the impact of your morning routine on productivity involves a combination of subjective self-assessments, objective metrics, regular reviews, and adaptability. By taking a holistic and systematic approach, you can gain actionable insights that empower you to make informed adjustments, leading to continuous improvement and sustained productivity. Tracking your progress, celebrating milestones, and staying adaptable will ensure that your morning routine remains a powerful tool for achieving both daily victories and long-term success.

Chapter 13: Adapting to Change

Every season of life brings its own challenges and opportunities, requiring us to adapt our routines accordingly. Embracing change, whether it's a shift in seasons, a new job, or unexpected life events, is crucial for maintaining a sense of balance and productivity. Instead of viewing change as a disruption, see it as a chance to evaluate what's working and what's not, and refine your morning routine to better serve your current needs. By staying flexible and open-minded, you can ensure that your morning rituals evolve in a way that supports your personal and professional growth. Remember, adaptability isn't about losing what works, but discovering ways to thrive no matter the circumstances.

Adjusting Your Routine for Different Seasons

As seasons change, so do the demands on our bodies and minds. Adapting your morning routine to accommodate these shifts can make a significant difference in maintaining productivity and well-being throughout the year. Recognizing the natural rhythm of the seasons and leveraging it can be a powerful way to stay aligned with your goals and keep your energy levels optimal.

In the bright and energetic days of summer, waking up early becomes easier for many. The early sunrise bathes your room in natural light, which can naturally nudge you out of bed. This is a prime time to engage in outdoor activities that might not be as accessible during colder months. Consider incorporating a morning jog, walk, or even a yoga session in your backyard.

These activities not only capitalize on the good weather but also give you an early boost of Vitamin D, enhancing your mood and energy levels.

On the flip side, winter mornings can be challenging. The shorter days and extended darkness sometimes make it hard to get out of bed. You might find yourself hitting the snooze button more often. To combat this, try making your mornings cozier and more inviting. Perhaps start with a warm cup of herbal tea or coffee, paired with five minutes of stretching to invigorate your body. Using a dawn simulator alarm clock, which gradually lightens your room, can mimic the natural rise of the sun and make waking up a bit easier.

Spring, often synonymous with renewal and growth, can be a fantastic season for setting new intentions and goals. The season's freshness and vitality can reflect in your routine with activities such as journaling or planning out new projects. It's a time to clear out the clutter, both mentally and physically. You might find it helpful to do a deep clean of your workspace or plan a digital detox to realign your focus.

Autumn provides a moment to reflect and prepare for the coming months. As the leaves change color and fall, it's a beckoning call to let go of what's not serving you and to ground yourself in what truly matters. Consider incorporating grounding practices such as meditation or mindful walks where you immerse yourself in the changing scenery. These moments of tranquil reflection can help you stay centered and resilient against the stresses that often come with the year's end.

Regardless of the season, your morning routine should cater to your environment and how it affects you personally. There's no one-size-fits-all approach, so pay attention to how your energy and mood fluctuate with the seasons. What works wonders in summer might not be as effective in winter. Being flexible and open to change ensures you remain productive and balanced throughout the year.

Of course, nutrition is another aspect to consider. In summer, lighter breakfasts such as smoothies or yogurt with fresh berries can keep you energized without feeling weighed down. During winter, hearty breakfasts like oatmeal with nuts, seeds, and a touch of honey can provide sustained energy and warmth. Seasonal produce can also play a huge role. Eating what's in season not only supports local agriculture but also ensures you're getting the freshest and most nutrient-rich foods available.

Exercise routines might also need adjustments. In warmer months, outdoor workouts can be invigorating, offering a change of scenery and an opportunity to breathe in fresh air. Conversely, winter might drive your workouts indoors, where you can engage in activities such as indoor cycling, home fitness apps, or even dance workouts. Remaining adaptable and keeping variety in your workouts will make it easier to stay consistent.

Additionally, your mental and emotional practices can benefit from seasonal tweaks. Summer might inspire more active, goal-setting kinds of mindsets, while winter might lean more toward introspection and gradual personal growth. Spring and autumn offer a balance – cultivating new seeds of habits in spring and harvesting the fruits of your labor in autumn.

When it comes to dress codes and prep time, different seasons have different demands. In winter, laying out your clothes the night before can save you precious minutes on chilly mornings. You might also prefer comfortable and cozy items to start your day off warmly. In summer, simpler and lighter clothing can ease your morning rush.

Bottom line, the key is intention. Adjusting your routine for different seasons requires intentionality and awareness. Regularly check in with yourself and assess what's working and what's not. Adjustments don't have to be drastic; small, incremental changes can make a profound impact over time. Embrace the ebb and flow of nature's cycles as part of your own journey towards greater productivity, health, and happiness.

Remember, even a well-designed routine requires flexibility. Life is dynamic, and so should be your approach to managing it. As you adapt to each new season, you'll build resilience and learn to flow with changes rather than resist them. This approach not only helps you optimize your productivity but also enriches your overall experience of life. After all, personal and professional growth often comes from how well we adapt to the world around us. So, infuse your mornings with the essence of the seasons, and let them guide you to a more balanced and fulfilling daily life.

CHAPTER 13: ADAPTING TO CHANGE

Coping with Unexpected Changes

Life is full of surprises. No matter how meticulous, organized, and consistent you are with your morning routine, unexpected changes can and will occur. How you respond to these disruptions is critical not only to maintaining productivity but also to nurturing your mental and emotional wellbeing. Knowing that you have strategies in place to cope with the unexpected can give you a sense of control and resilience, transforming what could be a stressful situation into an opportunity for growth and adaptation.

One of the first steps in coping with unexpected changes is adopting a mindset that embraces flexibility. A rigid approach to your morning routine might make it challenging to adapt when unforeseen events happen. Remember, the goal isn't to follow your routine perfectly every single day but to create a framework that enhances your life. When you maintain a flexible outlook, you can adapt your routine to fit the current circumstances without feeling like you've failed.

Consider developing a set of "backup" elements within your morning routine. Think of these as a simplified version of your usual activities that you can default to when time or resources are limited. For instance, if you normally dedicate 30 minutes to meditation, have a 5-minute version that you can quickly engage in when pressed for time. This way, you're not abandoning your routine altogether but modifying it to suit the day's demands.

Building resilience in the face of change also involves recognizing and managing your emotional reactions. When unexpected changes arise, it's easy to get frustrated or anxious. However, these emotions can cloud your judgment and derail your productivity. Instead, practice mindfulness techniques to stay grounded. Take a few deep breaths, acknowledge your feelings, and then let them pass. This practice helps you stay composed and focused, allowing you to handle the situation more effectively.

Another key aspect of coping with surprise disruptions is to *reframe your perspective*. Often, we view unexpected changes as obstacles, but they can also be opportunities for growth and learning. For example, if a last-minute meeting disrupts your morning routine, look at it as a chance to network or gain new insights that could be beneficial to your work. Adopting this positive mindset can transform your approach to challenges, making you more adaptable and resilient in the long run.

Communication is also crucial when dealing with unforeseen changes. Whether it's a family emergency, a sudden work task, or any other unexpected event, letting the relevant people know about your situation can ease the burden. Communicate your needs and limitations openly. If you're working with a team, inform them about the disruption and collaborate to find a solution. This transparency builds trust and fosters a supportive environment where everyone is more equipped to handle unexpected changes together.

One effective strategy for managing unexpected changes is to maintain a buffer period in your morning routine. Design your schedule with a bit of extra time built in around key activities. This buffer allows some wiggle room for handling interruptions without completely derailing your plans. For example, instead of back-to-back meetings, give yourself a 10-15 minute break to reset and refocus. This preparation can make a significant difference when the unexpected occurs.

In addition, having a well-organized and prioritized to-do list can be a lifesaver when disruptions occur. Knowing what tasks are essential and which can be postponed gives you the ability to quickly adjust your plans. Use productivity tools or apps that help you keep track of your priorities, and make it a habit to review and update your list regularly. This practice ensures that when an unexpected change happens, you can swiftly pivot and still meet your critical goals.

Emotional support is another important factor in navigating unexpected changes. It's okay to lean on friends, family, or colleagues when things go awry. Sharing your challenges and receiving support can be incredibly comforting and can provide you with new perspectives or solutions you hadn't considered. Don't hesitate to reach out for help or advice when you need it.

Finally, always keep the bigger picture in mind. A single disrupted morning or a minor setback doesn't define your overall progress. Look at your journey holistically. Acknowledge your achievements and understand that everyone faces disruptions. What matters is how you adapt and move forward. Real growth happens in the face of challenges, and your ability to cope with unexpected changes is a testament to your resilience and determination.

Life's unpredictability is a given, but by integrating flexibility, resilience, and effective strategies into your morning routine, you empower yourself to handle whatever comes your way. Embrace the unexpected as an opportunity rather than a hindrance, and you will find yourself not just surviving but thriving in the face of change.

Chapter 14: Technology and Minimalism

In our fast-paced, tech-driven world, the line between productivity and overwhelm can quickly blur. Embracing minimalism in the realm of technology is about making intentional choices that enhance your morning routine without succumbing to digital distractions. By stripping down to essential tools and apps that really add value, you create space for focus and clarity in your mornings. Try incorporating digital detox strategies like setting boundaries on screen time and curating your app usage to only those that support your goals. This balanced approach can transform your mornings, enabling you to harness the power of technology to aid productivity while maintaining a tranquil start to your day.

Digital Detox Strategies

As ambitious professionals and individuals striving for personal growth, it's essential to recognize the impact of incessant digital noise on our productivity and wellbeing. In our high-tech world, devices and notifications often dictate our lives, shrinking the gaps of silence and reflection we need to thrive. Enter the concept of digital detox: a planned, intentional break from screens and digital interference. To fully reap the benefits of technology and minimalism within your morning routines, adopting sustainable digital detox strategies can be a game-changer.

One effective way to begin a digital detox is by setting specific times during your day when all devices are off-limits. Establishing screen-free time slots can create pockets of calm and enhance your focus. Start small if the idea of long digital breaks seems intimidating. For instance, designate the first hour after waking up and the last hour before bed as device-free periods. Use this time to engage in mindful activities like journaling, meditating, or simply enjoying a quiet cup of coffee.

Removing phones and laptops from your bedside table is another powerful step. When our devices are within arm's reach, the temptation to check emails or social media feeds becomes almost irresistible. Invest in a good old-fashioned alarm clock and charge your devices in another room. This simple shift can drastically reduce your bedtime screen time and contribute to better sleep quality, setting a positive tone for the morning.

Another approach is to clean up your digital environment by decluttering your apps and notifications. Reduce the number of apps on your home screen to only the essentials. Disable push notifications for non-essential apps, and you'll find yourself less distracted by unnecessary dings and buzzes. This minimalistic approach can make your phone less of a constant intrusion and more of a purposeful tool.

During your morning routine, consider incorporating specific offline activities. Reading a physical book, engaging in a creative hobby, or taking a walk outside without your phone can be incredibly refreshing. These activities allow you to start the day grounded and centered, away from the relentless digital barrage.

Social media detoxes are particularly beneficial for mental clarity. Platforms designed to keep you hooked often lead to mindless scrolling, sapping your time and energy. Set specific blocks of time during the day to check social media, preferably after you've completed your most important morning tasks. Also, regularly reassess which accounts you follow—unfollow or mute any that don't inspire or uplift you.

Creating physical boundaries in your space can also foster a healthier digital relationship. Designate specific areas in your home as "no-tech zones," like the dining room or the bathroom. These boundaries can help create more meaningful, screen-free interactions, whether you're eating a meal or unwinding in the bath.

Another key strategy is mindfulness meditation, aimed at cultivating presence and awareness. Practicing mindfulness can help you become more conscious of your digital habits, empowering you to make deliberate choices about when and how you engage with technology. Start your day with a short meditation session, focusing on your breath or surroundings. This practice can set a tranquil tone for your morning and help you remain grounded throughout the day.

If your job requires you to be connected, try batching your digital tasks. Allocate specific times during the day to catch up on emails, messages, and other digital responsibilities. This way, you're not continually distracted by incoming alerts and can maintain a higher level of focus on the task at hand.

Time-blocking in conjunction with digital detox can bolster productivity significantly. By scheduling tech-free blocks in your calendar, you can prioritize deep work and creative tasks that require undisturbed focus. Consider aligning these blocks with your peak productivity hours to maximize their effectiveness.

A supportive environment can make a huge difference in your digital detox journey. Communicate your intentions with family members, friends, or colleagues. Let them know you're aiming for more intentional tech use and might not respond to messages or calls immediately. This can help manage expectations and foster a supportive network around your goals.

Creating a morning 'disconnection ritual' can be an inspiring way to commit to your digital detox. Make the act of turning off your devices a mindful practice, not just a mechanical process. Perhaps light a candle, play soothing music, or spend a few moments reflecting on what you want to achieve during your screen-free time. This ritualistic approach can transform the detox from a chore into a cherished part of your day.

It's also crucial to address any underlying anxieties about being disconnected. Fear of missing out or the need to be always available can drive excessive screen time. Cultivate trust in the process and remind yourself that the world won't fall apart if you take a few hours offline. Over time, as you realize the benefits, your anxiety will likely diminish.

Regularly reviewing and adjusting your digital habits is vital to maintaining a balanced relationship with technology. Like any habit, digital detox requires periodic reflection and tweaking. Use journaling or monthly reviews to assess what's working and what needs adjustment. Celebrate small victories and remain patient with the process.

Lastly, inspire yourself with success stories. Many high-achievers incorporate digital detox into their routines to enhance productivity and wellbeing. Learning about their strategies and experiences can provide motivation and practical tips. These tales of transformation can serve as powerful reminders of the benefits of managing your digital engagement consciously.

In a world where technology is omnipresent, reclaiming control over our digital lives is a vital aspect of achieving harmony between productivity and personal growth. By integrating these digital detox strategies into your morning routine, you're not just cutting down screen time; you're making a conscious choice to prioritize your mental clarity, focus, and overall wellbeing. So, seize the opportunity to disconnect, and watch how it transforms your mornings and your life.

Remember, the goal isn't to eliminate technology entirely but to use it in a way that serves you rather than enslaves you. With thoughtful implementation and consistency, these digital detox strategies can become a cornerstone of your journey towards a more balanced and fulfilling life.

Essential Morning Apps

Technology isn't typically the first thing you think of when merging the concepts of minimalism and purposeful living. Yet, when leveraged wisely, it can boost productivity and enhance well-being without overwhelming your morning routine. For ambitious professionals committed to personal growth, the right apps can be invaluable allies. In this chapter, we explore some essential morning apps that can help streamline your morning routines while maintaining a minimalistic approach.

Let's start with **wake-up and alarm apps**. Traditional alarms are blunt tools; they jolt you awake, often disrupting your sleep cycle. Apps like "Sleep Cycle" and "Alarmy" do more than just ring a bell. These apps use advanced algorithms to monitor sleep patterns and wake you up during the lightest phase of your sleep cycle, making waking up a less jarring experience. Starting the day smoothly can have a significant impact on your mood and energy levels throughout the day.

Another indispensable category is **meditation apps**. Apps like "Calm" and "Headspace" offer guided meditations that can help align your mental state right from the outset. Whether you have five minutes or half an hour, these apps can turn even the busiest mornings into moments of introspective calm. Studies have shown that regular meditation can reduce stress, improve concentration, and foster emotional resilience—all of which are valuable for professionals facing a hectic day ahead.

Next, consider **planning and productivity apps**. "Todoist" and "Trello" are fantastic tools for setting intentions and organizing daily tasks. Using these apps, you can create to-do lists, manage projects, and set priorities for the day. By having a solid plan in place, you're less likely to be sidetracked by distractions. Plus, checking off tasks as you complete them provides a satisfying sense of accomplishment, propelling you forward into the day.

For those keen on tracking their habits, **habit-tracking apps** like "Habitica" or "Streaks" can be a game-changer. These apps help you build and maintain good habits by visualizing progress and providing reminders. Whether you're aiming to drink more water, exercise, or read each morning, habit-tracking apps make it easier to stay accountable. They offer a methodical way to turn your aspirations into achievable, daily actions.

Nutrition and hydration apps are also crucial components of a morning routine aimed at wellness. "MyFitnessPal" and "WaterMinder" can guide you in making healthier food choices and ensuring adequate hydration. By logging your breakfast and tracking your water intake, you can make sure your body is fueled and ready to tackle the day's challenges. Proper nutrition and hydration are foundational to sustained energy and focus, essential for any ambitious professional.

Moreover, **news and information apps** like "Flipboard" and "Feedly" can be strategically used to keep you informed without overwhelming you with an endless stream of updates. Curating meaningful, relevant content ensures you're knowledgeable about your industry and the world, without the time sink of indiscriminate scrolling. These apps allow you to start your day smartly, ingesting only what aligns with your goals and interests.

Similarly, **learning and development apps** such as "Duolingo" or "Coursera" provide opportunities for personal and professional growth. You can spend a few minutes each morning learning a new language or acquiring new skills. This not only invigorates your brain but also sets a tone of continuous improvement and curiosity for the rest of the day. Education doesn't have to be a grand, time-consuming affair; even small, consistent efforts can yield significant long-term gains.

Mental health apps deserve a mention as well. Apps like "Moodpath" and "Happify" offer tools for managing your mental and emotional health. These apps often include mood trackers, therapeutic exercises, and mental health assessments that can guide you in maintaining emotional balance. For those aiming to be the best versions of themselves, acknowledging and attending to mental health is paramount.

Consider also **audiobook and podcast apps** like "Audible" and "Overcast." These apps bring a wealth of knowledge and inspiration to your fingertips—or rather, to your ears. Listening to a chapter of a motivational book or a thought-provoking podcast while you brew your morning coffee can be incredibly enriching. This is an excellent way to feed your mind while engaging in routine tasks, seamlessly combining personal development with daily activities.

One category of apps that often gets overlooked is **gratitude and journaling apps**. "Day One" and "Five Minute Journal" offer structured ways to reflect on what you're grateful for, set your intentions for the day, and jot down any thoughts or feelings. A few moments of journaling can provide clarity, focus, and a sense of purpose. It's a small practice that can yield immense benefits, fostering a positive mindset and greater self-awareness.

Let's not forget **minimalist productivity apps** like "Forest" and "Focus@Will." These apps help you minimize distractions and maintain focus on your tasks. "Forest," for instance, incentivizes you to stay off your phone by planting virtual trees that grow as you complete your tasks. "Focus@Will" offers music tracks scientifically designed to increase your focus and productivity. Balancing minimalism with productivity, these apps facilitate a more mindful, less cluttered approach to your daily responsibilities.

In conclusion, integrating technology into your morning routine doesn't have to conflict with a minimalist lifestyle. The key is to be selective and purposeful about the apps you choose. Each app mentioned serves a distinct, supportive role in enhancing your productivity, well-being, and personal growth. By employing these tools mindfully, you can craft a streamlined, effective morning routine that empowers you to bring your best self to each day.

Remember, it's not about how many apps you use, but how effectively you use them. Aim for simplicity and functionality, avoiding digital overload. This careful curation aligns perfectly with both productivity and minimalism principles, offering balance and harmony as you start your mornings. Choose wisely, use intentionally, and watch your mornings transform into a powerful launchpad for your day.

Chapter 15: Creating a Morning Playlist

Imagine your mornings infused with the perfect soundtrack, setting the stage for a day of productivity and positivity. A morning playlist can be a transformative tool, harnessing the power of music to elevate your mood, sharpen your focus, and energize your start. By carefully curating a selection of songs that resonate with your personal goals and emotions, you create a tailored auditory experience that aligns with your morning routine. Whether it's the soothing rhythms of instrumental music to ease into meditation or the upbeat, motivational tracks that get your blood pumping for a morning workout, the right playlist can make all the difference. Include a mix of genres and tempos to match various activities and emotional states you might encounter as you progress through your routine. Start experimenting with different tracks, noting which ones have the most profound impact on your energy levels and mindset. Soon, you'll find that your morning playlist isn't just background noise—it's a strategic part of your routine, driving you toward greater productivity and wellbeing each day.

The Benefits of Music

Integrating music into your morning routine can have profound benefits on your productivity and overall well-being. When chosen intentionally, the right playlist doesn't just sound good; it sets the stage for how you'll navigate the rest of your day. Music has a unique power to elevate your mood, boost your energy levels, and even improve cognitive function. For ambitious professionals and individuals keen on personal growth, leveraging these benefits can serve as an invaluable tool in crafting a morning that fuels success.

Starting your day with music can drastically improve your mood. Imagine waking up feeling groggy, dragging your feet to the bathroom, and forcing yourself through the motions. Now, replace that with the scenario where an upbeat, energizing playlist welcomes you as you step out of bed. The difference is palpable. Studies have shown that music triggers the release of dopamine, the brain's "feel-good" neurotransmitter. This chemical reaction can make you feel more optimistic and eager to take on the day's challenges.

Beyond mood enhancement, a well-curated morning playlist can sharpen your mental clarity and focus. Classical music, for instance, has been found to improve spatial-temporal skills, which are crucial for problem-solving and critical thinking. Conversely, instrumental tracks can eliminate the potential distractions of lyrics, allowing your brain to work more efficiently on tasks at hand. The genre and tempo of your music should align with your morning tasks—something slow and tranquil for meditation or light stretching, and something more upbeat for intensive workout routines.

Another significant benefit of incorporating music into your morning is that it can serve as a reliable cue in maintaining consistency in your routine. Pavlovian conditioning isn't just for dogs; humans, too, can create associations between sounds and actions. Listening to the same playlist each morning can signal your brain that it's time to wake up and start the day, thereby ingraining those habits deeper into your daily ritual. Before long, just hearing the opening notes of your first morning song can trigger a chain reaction of positive, productive behaviors.

In addition to immediate mental and emotional perks, the consistent use of morning music can yield long-term benefits for your physical health. Music has been proven to lower cortisol levels, the hormone responsible for stress. Lower cortisol levels mean less wear and tear on your body over time, contributing to better physical health and longevity. Moreover, engaging with music can help regulate heart rate and blood pressure, setting you up for a day where you're not just mentally alert but physically resilient.

For those worried about the time commitment required to create the perfect

CHAPTER 15: CREATING A MORNING PLAYLIST

morning playlist, there's good news. Many platforms offer pre-designed playlists tailored for various morning activities. Whether you need a collection of tranquil tunes for yoga or an energizing mix to power through a high-intensity interval training (HIIT) session, there's something for everyone. Additionally, the ease of access to curated playlists removes the guesswork, allowing you to effortlessly integrate this new element into your morning routine.

Imagine the compounded benefits when music becomes an integral part of your morning exercise routine. Music has been shown to enhance physical performance by increasing endurance, reducing perceived effort, and even providing a better rhythm for movements. Picture yourself running on a treadmill or doing a series of high-energy exercises, with each beat propelling you forward, each melody pushing you harder. Music's synchronicity with movement ensures you don't just go through the motions but fully engage in your physical activities.

When planning your morning playlist, it's essential to consider the tempo and mood of the tracks you're adding. Music that has a higher tempo (120-140 beats per minute) is great for activities that require more energy and movement, such as a morning jog or an intense workout. On the other hand, slower tracks or instrumental pieces can be perfect for meditation, stretching, or a calm, reflective start to your day. The goal is to match the energy of the music with the energy you want to manifest in each segment of your morning.

For parents juggling the morning chaos of getting kids ready for school, a family-friendly playlist can be a game-changer. When chosen thoughtfully, music can create a harmonious and joyful environment. Imagine transforming what usually feels like a stressful rush into a coordinated dance, with each family member moving through their tasks as the background music sets a positive tone. This not only improves the mood of the entire household but can also instill a sense of unity and shared purpose.

Even at work, the benefits of carrying a productive morning vibe are tangible. When you're accustomed to starting your day on a high note (pun intended), that momentum often carries through into your professional environment. Think about how much more effective meetings, brainstorming sessions, or even solo tasks could be when approached with a clear, motivated mind. The discipline of beginning your day with music-fueled focus can translate into higher productivity, better teamwork, and an overall enhanced work experience.

Beyond physical and cognitive benefits, music has the power to tap into deep emotional reservoirs, fostering a sense of gratitude and mindfulness. Certain songs and melodies evoke memories, stirring emotions that might otherwise remain dormant. By reviving these emotions each morning, you can cultivate a richer, more emotionally intelligent start to your day. This emotional vitality can spill over into interactions with colleagues, loved ones, and even strangers, creating a ripple effect of positivity and connection.

Workplace aside, a morning filled with music sets a tone of creativity and innovation. Artists, writers, and thinkers often cite music as a fundamental part of their creative process. Starting the day with music can eureka moments that might have otherwise remained buried under life's routine. Even if your profession is not traditionally "creative," a dose of creative energy can boost problem-solving abilities, making you more adept at navigating challenges and seizing opportunities.

Lastly, incorporating music into your morning routine can introduce a welcome element of fun and enjoyment. Sometimes, amidst the hustle to improve productivity and optimize routines, we lose sight of the joy in the process. Music brings an element of playfulness into your schedule, making the routine not just effective but also enjoyable. It's about creating a morning not just for achievement, but for well-rounded happiness and fulfillment.

In summary, the benefits of integrating music into your morning routine are multifaceted, touching on emotional, cognitive, and physical well-being. From boosting your mood and focus to enhancing physical performance and creating a positive atmosphere, music can transform mundane mornings into powerful launchpads for success. By thoughtfully curating your morning playlist, you can harness music's transformative power to not only fuel your ambitions but also enrich your daily life with joy and harmony.

CHAPTER 15: CREATING A MORNING PLAYLIST

Recommended Playlists

Music has an undeniable influence on our emotions and energy levels. A carefully curated playlist can act as a catalyst for success, setting the tone for your day, and propelling you towards your goals. When creating your morning playlist, remember: it's not just about what sounds good but also about what feels good. The right playlist can help you to combat morning grogginess and propel yourself into a state of heightened alertness and positivity.

To start, consider your personal tastes and preferences; what's energizing to one person may not be to another. Some people find upbeat pop or rock music incredibly motivating, while others might prefer classical pieces or instrumental tracks. The beauty of a personalized playlist is that it grows and changes with you.

Your first task is to identify music that resonates with your goals for the day. If you're aiming for productivity and mental clarity, songs with a steady rhythm and uplifting melodies can be particularly effective. Tracks that gradually build up can align well with the process of waking up and getting ready for the day. A musical arc can mimic your own need to transition from groggy to fully alert, providing a natural flow to your morning routine.

Incorporate motivational songs that have inspiring lyrics or themes. Words have power, and hearing empowering lyrics can set a positive tone for the day. These might include favorite tracks or even songs tied to memorable, uplifting experiences in your life. When you hear these tunes, they can evoke happy memories, making your morning much more enjoyable.

For those moments when you need to center yourself, consider adding in some slower-paced, calming music. It might be beneficial right after waking up or during a morning meditation session. Tracks with soft instrumental sounds or nature-inspired playlists can help you ease into the day smoothly, providing a brief respite before you dive into the hustle and bustle of your tasks.

A varied playlist helps keep things interesting. Transition between different genres throughout the week or even the morning. You might start with something slow and calming, building up to energizing tracks as you get into your morning exercise, and then perhaps something a bit more focused and steady as you move into work mode.

Also, don't underestimate the power of novelty. Regularly updating your playlist with new songs or different styles can keep your routine fresh and engaging. Getting bored with the same tunes means it's time to mix things up. Subscribe to curated playlists on streaming platforms; many of these are updated weekly and can introduce you to new artists and genres you might not discover otherwise.

Experiment with different sounds and observe how they impact your mood and energy levels. What uplifts you? What helps you focus? What makes you feel calm and centered? Use this self-awareness to refine your playlist continually.

In addition to individual songs and genres, consider the structure of your playlist. A good morning playlist isn't just a collection of uplifting tracks; it's sequenced to align with the stages of your morning routine. Tailor the beginning for wake-up contemplation, the middle for active engagements like exercise or showering, and the end for being more focused, aligning with planning or starting your work tasks.

For example, you might start with a gentle instrumental piece that allows you to wake up gradually. As you begin to move around and prepare breakfast, switch to something with a little more rhythm. During a morning workout, choose high-energy tracks that keep you motivated and moving. As you transition to planning your day, opt for tunes that are more neutral or even instrumental to avoid distraction.

Ultimately, a thoughtfully curated morning playlist is another form of preparation and intention-setting. It's about taking control of your environment to enhance your mindset. It's also an act of self-care, creating a ritual that not only boosts productivity but also adds joy to your routine. When you find the right combination of tunes, you'll notice the difference in how you feel and perform throughout the day.

Here are some examples to get you started:

- **Uplifting Pop:** Tracks by artists like Katy Perry, Bruno Mars, or Lizzo can

CHAPTER 15: CREATING A MORNING PLAYLIST

be incredibly energizing.
- **Classical Music:** Some people find that starting the day with pieces by Mozart, Beethoven, or Debussy helps improve focus and calm.
- **Instrumental and Chill:** Opt for lo-fi beats or smooth jazz which provides a pleasant background without overwhelming your senses.
- **Motivational Tracks:** Songs with inspiring lyrics, such as "Eye of the Tiger" by Survivor or "Just Like Fire" by P!nk.

Remember, the goal is to enhance your morning routine, making it invigorating and enjoyable. Being intentional with your morning playlist can be the soundtrack to a more productive, happier you. Start experimenting with different sounds, and watch how this simple addition can transform your mornings and, by extension, your days.

Chapter 16: Family and Social Considerations

Incorporating your family and social life into your morning routine is crucial for achieving a balanced and fulfilling lifestyle. It's not just about your personal growth, but also about creating a supportive environment that fosters collective wellbeing. Start by involving your family members in simple morning activities like stretching or having breakfast together. This shared time can strengthen your relationships and make the morning experience more enjoyable for everyone. Additionally, consider how social commitments—like meeting friends for a morning run or a quick coffee—can be harmoniously integrated into your routine without compromising your productivity goals. Balancing these aspects requires a combination of planning, open communication, and flexibility, but the rewards are manifold. You'll find that your morning routine not only empowers you to start the day with a sense of accomplishment but also nurtures your social bonds, making every day more meaningful and connected.

Involving Family Members

When it comes to creating and maintaining an effective morning routine, involving family members can be both rewarding and challenging. While personal productivity and wellbeing are the ultimate goals, recognizing that these objectives often intersect with family dynamics is crucial. By involving your family, you can foster a supportive environment where everyone benefits from the collective effort. Let's explore some ways to integrate family members into your morning routine without compromising individual goals.

First and foremost, family members can act as accountability partners. Knowing that someone else is aware of your goals can give you that extra push to stick with your routine. Share your plans and aspirations with your partner, children, or even roommates. By doing so, you create a supportive network that encourages consistent behavior and mutual growth. For instance, your spouse might remind you to drink water first thing in the morning, while you can encourage your children to start their day with a healthy breakfast.

Morning routines also offer a unique opportunity to strengthen familial bonds. Consider setting aside time for a group activity that everyone enjoys and benefits from. This could be a short walk around the neighborhood, a quick yoga session, or even a simple breakfast together. Such activities can instill a sense of togetherness and make mornings a more pleasant time for everyone. Children, especially, thrive on routines and shared experiences, so incorporating family-centric activities can be incredibly beneficial for their development.

For families with young children, mornings can often be chaotic. However, integrating your morning routine with their needs can bring a semblance of order to the morning hustle. Teach your children simple habits that can become part of their routine as well, such as making their beds, brushing their teeth, or preparing their school bags the night before. By doing this, you're not only easing your morning stress but also instilling valuable life skills in your children.

It's also important to acknowledge that each family member may have different goals and schedules. Flexibility is key. Allow each individual the space to prioritize their unique needs while still aiming for some overlap. For example, while one family member might enjoy a vigorous workout, another might prefer quiet meditation. Respecting these differences while maintaining a shared commitment to morning routines can help create a balanced environment that caters to everyone.

Communication is vital in this context. Have regular family meetings to discuss and refine your shared morning routine. These discussions can help address any obstacles and make adjustments as needed. In these meetings, encourage everyone to share what's working for them and what isn't. By being open and receptive to feedback, you'll create a routine that everyone can realistically commit to, making mornings more harmonious for all.

Additionally, technology can be a helpful tool in coordinating family routines. Utilize shared calendars or reminder apps to keep everyone on track. Setting up group reminders for activities or tasks can significantly increase adherence to the routine. Knowing that everyone is on the same page and actively participating can make the morning flow smoother and more enjoyable.

It's also beneficial to lead by example. Children, in particular, are very observant and tend to mimic the behaviors they see. By consistently sticking to your morning routine, you set a powerful example for them to follow. Demonstrate the importance of time management, self-care, and consistency through your actions. Over time, these lessons will resonate, and they'll naturally adopt similar habits into their own routines.

Mentally preparing for possible disruptions can also help you maintain your routine even when things don't go as planned. Life with family is inherently unpredictable—unexpected events, illnesses, or just a rough night's sleep can throw a wrench into your plans. Having a contingency plan can ensure that these disruptions don't completely derail your efforts. For instance, if your usual workout time gets interrupted, have a shorter, more flexible exercise routine as a backup.

Setting boundaries can be another critical aspect of involving family members in your morning routine. Respectfully communicate your need for undisturbed time if certain parts of your routine require solitude. Whether it's meditation, journaling, or reading, make it clear that these moments are important for your personal growth and should be respected. In turn, acknowledge and respect the individual needs and boundaries of other family members.

Inclusivity can also extend to extended family members who might not live with you but are part of your routine in other ways. Grandparents, for example, can be involved through video calls during breakfast or as part of a morning check-in to offer their wisdom and encouragement. This can create a multi-generational bond, enriching the morning routine with stories, advice, and emotional support.

Involving family members in your morning routine doesn't mean sacrificing your personal goals. Rather, it's about weaving those individual aims into a collective framework that benefits everyone. By fostering a supportive and adaptable environment, you create a morning routine that not only enhances productivity but also nurtures family connections. With open communication, flexibility, and mutual support, mornings can become a time of shared growth and well-being.

Balancing Social Commitments

Balancing social commitments with a rigorous morning routine might seem like a Herculean task, but it's all about finding harmony. For ambitious professionals, social engagements are often inevitable. Networking events, client dinners, and even casual weekend gatherings can easily fill up your calendar. The trick is to ensure that these social commitments add value to your life without derailing your morning plans.

One effective approach to maintaining this balance is by prioritizing. You don't need to attend every social event on your calendar. Learn to discern which ones are non-negotiable for your career or personal life and which you can afford to skip. Prioritize those that offer the most value, whether it's in terms of networking, personal relationships, or simply your wellbeing. By focusing on quality over quantity, you'll find that you have more energy and time to invest in your morning routine.

It's crucial to communicate your priorities to friends, family, and colleagues. If your morning routine is vital for your productivity and wellbeing, let them know. Most people will understand and may even admire your commitment to self-improvement. By setting clear boundaries, you protect your time without straining your relationships. Being upfront about your needs can create a more respectful and understanding social circle.

Of course, there will always be unforeseen social commitments that pop up.

Maybe you have friends visiting from out of town or an impromptu celebration. In such cases, flexibility becomes your ally. Allow yourself some room to adapt your routine. It's okay to adjust your wake-up time a little later after a late-night event, but try to stick to the essential parts of your routine that keep you grounded. This might mean a shorter workout or a quicker meditation session, but maintaining consistency, even in a reduced form, helps retain the habit.

Leveraging technology can also aid in balancing social commitments. Use digital calendars and planning apps to organize your social engagements. Tools like shared calendars can help you and your partner align your schedules, making it easier to see how social events fit into your overall plan. When you can visualize your week ahead, it's easier to carve out dedicated time for your morning routine and still honor your social commitments.

Additionally, combine social engagements with elements of your morning routine whenever possible. If you enjoy jogging, invite a friend to join you in the morning. Not only do you maintain your exercise routine, but you also nourish your social interactions. Combining activities can be a powerful way to adhere to your morning habits while staying socially active.

Furthermore, don't underestimate the power of saying "no." It's a simple word but incredibly effective in preserving your time. While it might be uncomfortable initially, learning to decline invitations graciously can give you the space needed to focus on what truly matters. Phrases like "I have a prior commitment" or "I need some personal time" are respectful ways to turn down invitations without offending others.

Establishing a rhythm can also be beneficial. For instance, allocate specific days of the week for social activities. This way, you can map out the rest of your week around these engagements. By having a predictable pattern, you're not constantly reshuffling your schedule, making it easier to maintain your morning routine.

Balance doesn't mean equal parts but rather the right mix that suits your lifestyle. It means giving yourself permission to enjoy a night out without guilt and waking up the next day and diving back into your routine. It's about understanding that social connections are an integral part of a fulfilling life but so is your personal growth and productivity.

Lastly, reflect on your social engagements periodically. Are they leaving you energized or drained? The ones that consistently leave you feeling revitalized are worth keeping. In contrast, those that deplete your energy may require reevaluation. Self-reflection helps in fine-tuning your social calendar to make way for a morning routine that empowers you.

In summary, balancing social commitments is an ongoing practice of prioritization, communication, flexibility, and self-awareness. It's about molding your social life to support your goals rather than letting it impede your progress. With practice, you'll find a rhythm that harmonizes both aspects of your life, enabling you to thrive both personally and socially.

Chapter 17: Weekend Routines

Weekends are a golden opportunity to either reinforce your morning routines or to give yourself some much-needed rest and rejuvenation. Tailoring your mornings to include a little extra leisure can be equally powerful in enhancing your overall productivity and well-being. Aim to strike a balance—start your day with light yet invigorating activities, such as a leisurely walk or some gentle yoga. Pour time into hobbies that ignite your passion but often fall by the wayside during a hectic workweek. Keep in mind, too, the importance of social connections; a relaxed brunch with family or friends can do wonders for your emotional health. By making your weekend routines both restorative and fulfilling, you're setting yourself up to hit the ground running when Monday rolls around.

Tailoring Your Weekend Mornings

As ambitious professionals, your weekdays might be governed by strict schedules and deadlines. However, weekends offer a unique opportunity to break free from that rigidity and personalize your mornings in ways that not only prepare you for the upcoming week but also enhance your overall wellbeing.

First, it's essential to recognize that weekday routines can differ vastly from weekend ones. While consistency is key to forming solid habits, allowing yourself some flexibility on the weekends can be hugely beneficial. This balance between structure and freedom is crucial for maintaining both productivity and mental health.

Imagine waking up to a weekend morning without the relentless buzz of alarms, where you give yourself the grace to wake up naturally. However, this doesn't mean oversleeping. Find that sweet spot where you can wake up feeling refreshed yet not overly indulgent. Aim for a time that's later than your usual weekday alarm but still early enough to capitalize on the calm and quietude of the morning hours.

Once you're up, incorporate mindful practices that set a relaxed yet intentional tone for the day. This might mean starting your morning with some light stretching or yoga. As Chapter 6 will delve deeper into the benefits of morning workouts, the weekend serves as an excellent time for a gentler, more reflective form of exercise that focuses on enhancing your flexibility and tranquility.

Nutrition, covered comprehensively in Chapter 5, is equally critical during weekends. Weekday mornings might force you into grabbing a quick bite, but weekends invite you to savor your breakfast. Opt for meals that are both nourishing and enjoyable. Perhaps try out that new recipe you've been curious about or indulge in a leisurely brunch. The key is to treat yourself without derailing your nutritional goals.

Weekend mornings are also an opportune time for mental and emotional rejuvenation. Utilizing journaling techniques, as discussed in Chapter 7, can help in reflecting on your week, setting intentions, or simply unloading your mind. Writing down your thoughts can offer astonishing clarity and pave the way for more focused weekdays.

Additionally, consider dedicating some time to reading or listening to audiobooks, enhancing your personal development journey which we explore further in Chapter 9. Weekends provide a stress-free window to immerse yourself in books that inspire and educate you. This practice not only feeds your mind but can also equip you with fresh perspectives and ideas to integrate into your professional life.

Planning and setting intentions should not be confined to weekdays alone. Chapter 8 elaborates on daily planning techniques, but the weekend offers you a chance to plan from a more detached vantage point. Reflect on not just your day but your entire week. What did you achieve? Where did you fall short? Use these moments to strategize and set actionable goals for the upcoming week. Coupled with affirmations, this practice sets a positive tone and builds a resilient mindset.

Rest is just as vital as productivity, and weekends are perfect for recalibrating your energy levels. Chapter 10's insights into the role of sleep are essential for understanding how to leverage weekends to catch up on rest without oversleeping. Prioritize sleep hygiene practices to ensure the quality of your rest is as beneficial as the length.

Incorporating family or social activities into your weekend mornings can significantly contribute to your emotional wellbeing. While weekdays might limit your time for such engagements, the more relaxed pace of weekend mornings allows you to connect with loved ones. Shared breakfasts, morning walks, or simple conversations can strengthen your social bonds and enhance your overall happiness. This is a theme we'll revisit in Chapter 16, focusing on balancing these commitments seamlessly.

Finally, weekends are a fantastic time to delve into creative or leisurely activities that you might not have time for during the week. Whether it's painting, cooking, gardening, or any hobby that rejuvenates your spirit, these activities can positively impact your mood and creativity.

If technology often dominates your weekdays, consider implementing some digital detox strategies on weekend mornings. Chapter 14 will explore this topic further, but for now, think about starting your day screen-free. Replace your phone-checking habit with a more mindful activity like reading, meditating, or simply enjoying your breakfast without distractions.

The essence of tailoring your weekend mornings lies in balancing relaxation with intention. It's about embracing a slower pace without losing sight of your goals. Use this time to reenergize your body, mind, and soul so that you step into your week feeling prepared and motivated.

Ultimately, your weekend mornings are a canvas for crafting those moments of relaxation, reflection, and preparation that can propel you towards achieving your long-term ambitions. Take this opportunity to explore and adapt practices that resonate with you, and watch how a tailored weekend routine can transform not just your weekends, but your entire week ahead.

Rest and Recreation

The weekend unfurls like a soft, welcoming blanket after a week of relentless work and dedication. It's a time when the ambitious professional, so keen on productivity and personal growth, can find moments of rest and recreation that reenergize the spirit and sharpen the mind for the week ahead. But rest and recreation are not merely activities; they are essential components of a balanced life, directly impacting how effective your morning and daily routines can be.

You've meticulously crafted a morning routine that supercharges your weekdays, but weekends demand a different approach. This is the time to hit pause, recharge your batteries, and indulge in the simple joys that often get sidelined. This chapter reveals how you can optimize your weekends for recovery while still retaining that sense of purpose and progression.

Recreation isn't just about "having fun". It's an essential part of personal growth. Think of it as a necessary recalibration for your mind and body. It's the perfect antidote to workweek stressors and can provide you with a fresh perspective. For instance, hobbies like painting, gardening, or even cooking can offer a form of active meditation. Engaging in recreational activities helps disengage the logical part of your brain and gives the creative and emotional parts some breathing room.

Imagine the satisfaction of completing a puzzle, or the thrill of learning a new skill. Recreation can be invigorating. Andreas, a project manager, swears by weekend hiking trips. "It's not just the physical aspect. It's about connecting with nature, which clears my mind in ways that no amount of planning or strategizing at work can." This renewed clarity isn't incidental. Nature, with its boundless beauty, brings us face to face with the wonders we've neglected to appreciate.

Your weekend mornings hold incredible potential. It's tempting to sleep in, and while catching a few extra Zs can be beneficial, structuring your weekend mornings with a blend of rest and recreation sets a positive tone for the entire day. Begin your day with a leisurely but nutritious breakfast. Experiment with new recipes you've fancied during the week but never had time to try.

One might think "recreation" means filling your weekend with activity after activity. However, the true essence of rejuvenation lies in finding a balance between activity and relaxation. Yes, engage in your hobbies, but also take the time for rest. Quality rest can be as potent as any productivity hack. It's more than just physical rest; it's mental and emotional decompression. A Saturday morning spent lounging with a book or watching a documentary can be incredibly refreshing.

For professionals who are on their feet all week, consider incorporating gentle physical activities. Yoga, light stretching, or even a walk in the park can aid in alleviating the bodily stress accumulated during the week. Physical recreation doesn't have to be intense; it should be pleasurable and healing.

Additionally, weekends are a splendid opportunity for social recreation. Involve your friends and family in your activities. Shared experiences foster deeper connections and provide a robust support system. Nathan, a young executive, shares his weekend recreation tips. "Saturday afternoons, I gather a group of friends for a casual soccer game. It's a fun workout, and the camaraderie really helps me unwind."

Moreover, mental and emotional recreation is vital. Puzzles, board games, or even meditative practices can activate your brain's reward system, providing a sense of achievement and relaxation simultaneously. Create a playlist of your favorite tunes or dive into a podcast that you've been meaning to explore. Preston, a software engineer, finds solace in his weekend routine of listening to a new album with his morning coffee. "It's become a ritual. Music helps set the emotional tone for my day," he explains.

If you're finding it hard to detach from work, designate specific hours or a full day as a "no-work zone". This separation ensures that your mind can genuinely unwind and recover. Digital detoxes are particularly effective. Allocate some time to disconnect from emails, social media, and other digital engagements. A few hours away from screens can do wonders for mental clarity and focus.

It's equally crucial to listen to your body and mind. Some weekends, you might feel the need for complete rest. That's okay. Allow yourself the grace to have a lazy afternoon nap or a movie binge. Rest shouldn't feel like an indulgence; it's a necessity.

Understand that the quality of your weekend rest and recreation directly contributes to the efficiency of your weekday routines. Consider it an investment in your productivity. A refreshed mind approaches tasks with greater creativity and resilience. A well-rested body endures the demands of the workweek with more vigor and less strain.

When Sunday evening rolls around, wind down thoughtfully. Reflect on your weekend, acknowledge what brought you joy, and prepare mentally for the week ahead. Creating a short, calming evening routine can bridge the gap between weekend relaxation and the upcoming workweek. Whether it's journaling, a soothing bath, or a quiet cup of tea, these activities signal to your mind that it's time to transition back into "productive mode".

Implementing these strategies doesn't require drastic changes. Start small. If you've spent weekends in perpetual motion or lounging aimlessly, it's time to introduce a balance of rest and recreation consciously. Over time, these simple adjustments will become second nature, enriching your weekends and fortifying your weekday routines.

Ultimately, rest and recreation are about giving yourself permission to enjoy life amidst your ambitions. By embracing these moments, you are not only caring for your current well-being but also laying the groundwork for sustained personal and professional growth. Your weekend routines should leave you feeling rejuvenated and ready to conquer the week ahead, armed with renewed energy and a zest for accomplishment.

Chapter 18: Morning Routines for Different Personalities

Understanding that we're all wired differently is crucial in crafting a morning routine that feels genuinely transformative rather than just another task on a to-do list. For introverts, a serene, solitary start to the day might include activities like journaling, meditation, or reading—time to reflect inwardly and nurture their inner world before stepping into social environments. Extroverts, on the other hand, might find energy in starting their day with dynamic activities like a group workout, engaging in lively music, or morning calls with friends to spark motivation. Tailoring your routine to fit your personality can be the key to unlocking a morning that sets you up for success, leveraging your natural inclinations to fuel your productivity and wellbeing.

Tailoring Routines for Introverts

Tailoring a morning routine specifically for introverts can significantly enhance their productivity, well-being, and overall sense of fulfillment. Introverts recharge by spending time alone, and therefore, it's crucial to build a morning routine that respects this need for solitude. By doing so, they can start their day feeling grounded and energized.

The first step in crafting an introvert-friendly morning routine is to create a quiet environment. If you share your living space, consider waking up earlier than others to enjoy some peaceful moments alone. Use this time to engage

CHAPTER 18: MORNING ROUTINES FOR DIFFERENT PERSONALITIES

in activities that foster inner peace and mental clarity, such as meditation or reflective journaling. These practices help introverts center themselves and set a positive tone for the day.

Meditation, in particular, offers profound benefits for introverts. A few minutes of deep breathing and mindfulness can clear the mind and reduce anxiety. Start with short sessions and gradually increase the duration as you become more comfortable. Use a dedicated space free from distractions to practice meditation. This regular routine can serve as an anchor, bringing a sense of stability and calm to the rest of your day.

Journaling is another powerful tool for introverts. The act of writing down thoughts, goals, and reflections can provide clarity and emotional release. Choose a quiet corner, grab your favorite journal, and let your thoughts flow freely. Whether you're setting daily intentions, reflecting on past experiences, or simply noting down things you're grateful for, journaling allows introverts to process their inner world in a structured way.

In addition to meditative and reflective practices, consider incorporating creative activities into your morning. Introverts often have rich inner lives and may find expression through art, writing, or music. Engaging in a creative pursuit first thing in the morning can be incredibly fulfilling and set a positive, productive tone for the rest of the day. Whether it's writing a few pages of a novel, sketching, or playing a musical instrument, these activities can be both grounding and inspiring.

Another essential aspect for introverts is minimizing overstimulation. This might mean limiting exposure to news or social media in the early hours. Instead, substitute these with activities that you find calming and enjoyable. For instance, reading a book that inspires or motivates you can be a fantastic way to kickstart your day without the external noise and distraction.

Physical activity, albeit gentle, can also be beneficial. Activities like yoga or stretching exercises are particularly suited for introverts as they promote relaxation and mindfulness. Engage in a series of slow, deliberate movements that not only wake up your body but also quiet your mind. If preferred, a solitary walk in nature can provide the dual benefits of physical exercise and mental solitude, allowing for moments of quiet reflection and rejuvenation.

It's also important to plan your day ahead. Introverts thrive on structure and having a clear plan can reduce the uncertainty that might lead to stress. Dedicate a few minutes each morning to outline your key priorities and tasks. This can be as simple as making a list in a planner or using a digital tool to map out your day. Knowing what to expect can help you mentally prepare and approach tasks with a clear, focused mind.

While planning, don't forget to schedule breaks throughout your day. Introverts need time to recharge, so it's essential to create pockets of solitude between demanding tasks or social interactions. These breaks can be brief moments of silence, a walk around the block, or even a necessary escape to a quiet room. Recognizing and honoring the need for these breaks can significantly improve your well-being and sustain energy levels over the day.

Incorporating grounding rituals into your morning routine can be a game-changer. This might involve enjoying a warm cup of tea while you watch the sunrise, practicing gratitude, or engaging in a calm hobby like gardening. The objective is to engage in something that makes you feel connected to yourself and the world in a gentle, nurturing way.

Finally, consistency is key. Building a morning routine that you can maintain is crucial for long-term benefits. Start with small, manageable changes and gradually expand them over time. An effective routine isn't about cramming in as many activities as possible; it's about quality and what personally resonates with you. A consistent, well-tailored morning routine helps reinforce the habits that contribute to your overall productivity and satisfaction.

In summary, tailoring a morning routine for introverts involves creating a peaceful, structured environment that emphasizes solitude, creativity, and mindfulness. By incorporating practices like meditation, journaling, gentle physical activity, and planned reflections, you can craft a morning routine that not only fits your personality but also sets a positive tone for your entire day. With consistent practice, these habits can lead to greater productivity, emotional resilience, and a deep sense of personal fulfillment.

CHAPTER 18: MORNING ROUTINES FOR DIFFERENT PERSONALITIES

Tailoring Routines for Extroverts

Extroverts thrive on social interaction and external stimulation. Understanding this key trait is crucial for designing an effective morning routine that aligns with their intrinsic motivations. Unlike introverts who may find solitude energizing, extroverts draw their energy from engaging with others. As such, tailoring morning routines for extroverts can deeply impact their day, setting a positive and dynamic tone from the moment they wake up.

One of the most effective strategies for an extrovert's morning routine is incorporating social activities early in the day. This could be something as simple as arranging a coffee chat with a friend or colleague. Social connections not only provide a burst of positive energy but also establish a supportive network to start the day. A quick call or a video chat can often empower an extrovert, enhancing their productivity and emotional wellbeing.

Another vital element is community-based exercise. Whether it's a group fitness class, a morning run with a neighbor, or participating in a local sports league, physical activity combined with social interaction can catapult an extrovert's energy levels. Engaging in exercise with others fosters accountability and transforms a solitary workout into a fun, social experience. Physical activity also releases endorphins, bolstering the mood and setting a powerful precedent for the day ahead.

For professionals, networking breakfasts or early morning meetings can offer dual benefits of productivity and social engagement. Scheduling work interactions in the morning aligns with the extrovert's natural inclinations, making leadership meetings, brainstorming sessions, or collaborative projects more fluid and dynamic. This approach not only improves individual performance but also fosters a collaborative team environment. The key is to leverage the extrovert's innate tendency to flourish in social settings to enhance work outcomes.

Extroverts may also benefit from integrating technology in their morning routine to simulate social interactions. Engaging in social media platforms, watching motivational videos, or listening to podcasts that involve dialogues or interviews can inject a sense of connection and engagement right from the start. These activities provide a blend of social stimulation and inspirational content, fueling both the social and intellectual fires of an extrovert.

It's equally important for extroverts to plan their morning with flexibility and variety. In addition to scheduled activities, leaving room for spontaneous interactions can prove beneficial. For example, a quick chat with a neighbor during a morning walk or a visit to a bustling coffee shop can provide the unplanned social engagement that extroverts often crave. Such spontaneous moments can be refreshing breaks that keep the rigid structure of a routine dynamic and exciting.

Morning routines for extroverts should also place a strong emphasis on communication. Whether it's jotting down thoughts in a journal or verbally affirming daily goals and intentions, articulating ideas can significantly enhance clarity and focus. Many extroverts find that expressing thoughts out loud or discussing plans with someone helps in organizing their day more efficiently. This practice blends the benefits of self-reflection with the extrovert's need for communication.

Another engaging practice for extroverts is mindfulness through active engagement. Traditional methods of meditation might feel isolating, but alternatives like guided group meditations or yoga sessions can provide the calming benefits of mindfulness within a social context. Activities that allow for both inward reflection and outward connection provide a balanced approach to mental and emotional wellbeing.

Creating a morning playlist filled with energizing music is another tailor-made ritual for extroverts. Music has the power to elevate mood and set the tone for the day. Curate a collection of songs that are both uplifting and energizing, boosting positivity and enthusiasm. Playing this playlist while preparing breakfast or during a morning workout can amplify the overall impact of the routine.

Utilizing affirmations and positive self-talk can also be particularly powerful for extroverts. Standing in front of a mirror and verbally reinforcing goals and capabilities can build confidence and set a resilient mindset. This practice is more than just a confidence booster; it's a way to channel the extrovert's communicative energy into motivating outcomes, strengthening focus and

CHAPTER 18: MORNING ROUTINES FOR DIFFERENT PERSONALITIES

intention throughout the day.

Balancing the social aspects of a morning routine with moments of solitude is crucial for sustainability. Even for extroverts, brief periods of uninterrupted time can enhance productivity and creativity. Consider setting aside a few minutes for individual tasks like reading or planning, providing a balanced rhythm that prevents burnout despite high levels of social interaction.

Finally, extroverts can enhance their morning routines by incorporating gratitude practice in a social context. Sharing daily gratitude lists with friends, family, or colleagues can foster not only personal reflection but also deepen social bonds. Starting the day with a sense of appreciation magnified through shared experiences can greatly influence overall contentment and motivation.

In conclusion, tailoring morning routines to the extrovert's natural tendencies involves a thoughtful blend of social interaction, physical activity, and flexible planning. By aligning with their intrinsic motivations for external stimulation and communication, extroverts can start their days fully energized and ready to conquer professional and personal goals. This holistic approach ensures that their mornings not only jumpstart productivity but also enhance overall wellbeing.

Chapter 19: The Role of Environment

The environment you wake up to plays a crucial role in the success of your morning routine. Imagine stepping into a serene, clutter-free space where everything has its place; this sets a tone of tranquility and readiness. Organizing your morning environment isn't just about aesthetics; it's about creating a landscape conducive to focus and productivity. Think about the lighting, the sounds, and even the scent in your space. Crafting a peaceful environment lets you take control of your day right from the get-go. By eliminating distractions and fostering a positive atmosphere, you prepare yourself mentally and physically for the challenges ahead, setting a strong foundation for a proactive and fulfilling day.

Creating a Peaceful Space

A peaceful space acts as the foundation for any successful morning routine. The environment you create can significantly influence your mindset, productivity, and overall wellbeing. Crafting a sanctuary that promotes tranquility and focus is not just about physical surroundings but also about the psychological impact it holds. Let's explore how you can design a space that becomes an anchoring point for your morning routine.

First things first: declutter. A clean and organized space reduces distractions and stress, allowing you to concentrate on your intentions for the day. Start by getting rid of items that no longer serve a purpose. When your environment is clutter-free, it becomes easier to clear your mind too. Remember, simplicity fosters serenity. Even if you're a maximalist at heart,

CHAPTER 19: THE ROLE OF ENVIRONMENT

finding a balance between personal style and orderliness can create a more calming atmosphere.

The next step involves incorporating elements that stimulate the senses positively. Think about the textures, colors, and scents that bring you joy and relaxation. Lush green plants can enhance air quality and offer a touch of nature's calmness. Soft fabrics and comfy seating arrangements will invite you to sit, reflect, and set your daily intentions. Pay attention to your color scheme—cool tones like blues and greens often promote peace and focus, while warmer colors like yellows and oranges can energize you.

Now, consider lighting. Natural light is a tremendous boost to your mood and energy levels. If possible, position your morning space near a window where sunlight floods in. Invest in light-filtering curtains to control glare while maintaining the benefits of natural light. When natural light isn't an option, opt for full-spectrum bulbs that mimic daylight. Smart lighting systems that adjust between cool and warm tones can also help sync your artificial lighting to the natural rhythms of the day.

Sound can play an enormous role in creating a peaceful space as well. Everyone has different auditory preferences, so it's important to find what works for you. Perhaps the gentle hum of a white noise machine or a playlist of soothing nature sounds sets the right tone. On the other hand, complete silence might be what you need to center yourself. Tailor your sound environment to match your morning goals, whether that's relaxation, focus, or a combination of both.

Scent is another powerful tool for setting the mood. You might add essential oils known for their relaxing properties to a diffuser; consider lavender for tranquility or citrus scents for an invigorating start to the day. Avoid overpowering smells that could become a distraction. The goal is to create an olfactory backdrop that enhances your morning routine without drawing focus away from your tasks.

While the physical aspects are vital, the emotional and psychological resonance of your space can't be overlooked. A space filled with positive energy often promotes a better mindset. Display items that inspire you— photos, art, quotes, or mementos. Use visual reminders of your goals and dreams to keep you motivated. When you surround yourself with things that bring you joy, you create an environment that fosters positivity and productivity.

Integrating rituals into your peaceful space can also deepen your morning experience. This could be something as simple as lighting a candle, sipping your favorite tea, or reading a few pages of an inspirational book. The act of performing these rituals in a space designed for peace will elevate your routine, making it more meaningful and enjoyable. Rituals build a sense of stability and comfort, adding layers of intention to your mornings.

Digital devices are a double-edged sword when it comes to creating a peaceful space. While they offer convenience, they also bring potential distractions. Decide if and how you will incorporate technology into your morning haven. If you choose to have electronic devices, consider setting them to airplane mode or utilizing apps that promote mindfulness over mindless scrolling. Alternatively, this space might be a tech-free zone, encouraging you to unplug and focus inwardly before diving into the demands of the digital world.

Lastly, keeping your space versatile can prove advantageous. You might need an area that adapts to different activities throughout your morning routine. For example, a corner that serves as a meditation spot can also be used for stretching exercises or quiet reading. Flexibility ensures that your peaceful space remains functional, accommodating various aspects of your routine without causing disruption or confusion.

Creating a peaceful space is not an overnight task but a continuous process of fine-tuning and adjustment. As your needs and preferences evolve, so should your environment. Stay attuned to how your space makes you feel, and be willing to make changes that enhance your morning routine. After all, this is your sanctuary, a place where you can reconnect with yourself, set intentions, and start each day on a positive note.

Remember, the goal is to build an environment that nurtures you. A well-thought-out space can serve not only as a physical anchor but also as a mental and emotional beacon, guiding you towards becoming the best version of yourself. When you prioritize creating a peaceful space, you set the stage for a morning routine that is both productive and fulfilling.

Organizing Your Morning Environment

Creating an effective morning routine isn't just about what you do; it's also about where you do it. The environment you wake up to can set the tone for your entire day. Just as a cluttered desk can lead to a cluttered mind, an unorganized morning space can derail even the best-laid plans. Let's dive into how you can optimize your morning environment for maximum productivity and wellbeing.

First and foremost, consider the lighting in your space. Exposure to natural light can significantly influence your mood and alertness. If possible, allow natural light to flood your room by opening curtains or blinds as soon as you wake up. If natural light is scarce, invest in a high-quality wake-up light that mimics sunrise. These devices gradually brighten over a set period, nudging you into a gentle and natural wakefulness. The key is to create an environment that tells your brain it's time to start the day.

The organization of your physical space is equally crucial. Begin by decluttering your bedroom and bathroom. A tidy space can help mitigate the chaos that often accompanies the rush of morning activities. Utilize storage solutions like drawers, baskets, and shelves to keep essential items accessible but out of sight. Make your bed immediately after waking up; this small act of organization can provide a sense of accomplishment and set a positive tone for the day.

Another element to consider is the ambiance. Incorporate elements that soothe and inspire you. Aromatherapy diffusers with essential oils like lavender or eucalyptus can create a calming atmosphere. Select a few meaningful pieces of art or photographs that ignite a sense of joy or motivation when you see them. These elements can transform your morning from a monotonous routine into a rejuvenating ritual.

Temperature control is also an unsung hero of a productive morning environment. An optimal room temperature can facilitate a smoother transition from rest to activity. According to sleep experts, the ideal bedroom temperature for sleep—and consequently for waking up—hovers around 60-67 degrees Fahrenheit. Experiment with different temperatures to find what makes you most comfortable and alert in the morning.

Noise levels play a pivotal role as well. Start your day with sounds that promote relaxation and focus. Whether it's the serene notes of a morning playlist or the ambient sounds of nature, allow these auditory cues to ease you into wakefulness. If you live in a noisy environment, consider investing in noise-canceling headphones or white noise machines to create a tranquil space for your morning routine.

Now, let's talk about your workspace if you start your day with work or any form of productivity. A dedicated workspace equipped with all the tools you need can streamline your tasks and eliminate unnecessary stress. Arrange your desk to include essentials like a notepad, pens, a planner, and, if needed, electronic devices that are fully charged. A clean, organized desk will invite you to sit down and start working, rather than dreading the chaos.

It's also vital to consider ergonomics. Poor posture and uncomfortable furniture can lead to physical discomfort, which can be a substantial distraction. Invest in a good quality chair that provides adequate support and, if possible, a desk that can be adjusted for sitting or standing. Ergonomically designed furniture can dramatically improve your focus and productivity, making it worth the investment.

Moreover, setting boundaries within your morning environment can help maintain focus. If you share your space with family or roommates, communicate your need for a quiet, uninterrupted period in the mornings. Establishing and respecting these boundaries can create a buffer, safeguarding your productive time. It may be challenging at first, but consistency will help others understand and respect your morning routine.

Incorporating plants into your morning area can have several benefits. Not only do they purify the air, but they also create a soothing, natural vibe. Studies have shown that interacting with plants can reduce stress and boost your mood. Select low-maintenance plants like succulents or snake plants that require minimal care but still offer a host of benefits.

Your choice of morning attire plays its part, too. Laid-back but purposeful

CHAPTER 19: THE ROLE OF ENVIRONMENT

clothing can affect your psychological readiness to tackle the day. Even if you're working from home or spending a quiet morning reading, wearing something that's comfortable yet polished can positively influence your mindset. Set out your clothes the night before to simplify your morning choices and save valuable time.

The benefits of organizing your morning environment aren't merely practical; they're deeply psychological. A well-structured space can embody the intentions you set for your day, turning abstract goals into tangible actions. This alignment between your environment and your aspirations can make all the difference in maintaining consistency and achieving long-term success.

Remember, organizing your morning environment is an ongoing process. What works for you today might need tweaking tomorrow. Periodically reassess your space and routines to ensure they continue to meet your needs and support your objectives. Flexibility and adaptability are key to creating an environment that evolves with you, helping you meet the ever-changing demands of your life.

In summary, taking the time to create an organized, inviting, and functional morning environment can have profound impacts on your daily productivity and overall well-being. From lighting and temperature control to decluttering and personalizing your space, these adjustments can transform the way you start each day. As you embark on this journey, remember that the goal isn't perfection but progress. Each small change brings you one step closer to a morning environment that fuels your best self.

Chapter 20: Overcoming Common Challenges

As you forge ahead in establishing your morning routine, it's inevitable that you'll encounter obstacles. Whether it's the pervasive lure of procrastination or the struggle to shake off morning fatigue, these challenges can threaten to derail your progress. However, understanding that these hurdles are part of the journey is crucial. Embrace the process of overcoming them by experimenting with different strategies—such as setting smaller, achievable goals to combat procrastination or incorporating a brief, invigorating exercise session to battle grogginess. Remember, the key is persistence. By viewing these challenges as opportunities for growth rather than impediments, you'll build the resilience needed to maintain and elevate your morning routine over time.

Dealing with Procrastination

Procrastination is the silent saboteur of many ambitious professionals, stealthily eroding their productivity and thwarting their personal growth. It doesn't announce its presence with a crash but sneaks into your day, disguised as delays and distractions, until you find yourself wondering where the hours went. Dealing with procrastination effectively can be a game-changer when it comes to enhancing your morning routine and overall productivity.

Understanding the root cause of procrastination is the first step towards addressing it. Often, it's not just about laziness or poor time management. It

CHAPTER 20: OVERCOMING COMMON CHALLENGES

can stem from fear of failure, perfectionism, or simply feeling overwhelmed by the task at hand. Identifying why you procrastinate can provide powerful insights into how to combat it. For example, if fear of imperfection is your nemesis, adopting a mindset that values progress over perfection can be liberating. Remember, done is better than perfect.

Breaking tasks into smaller, more manageable pieces can also help in tackling procrastination. When a task feels too big, it's easy to postpone it because it seems insurmountable. By dividing it into smaller steps, you make it more approachable and less intimidating. Start with the simplest part and gradually build momentum. This approach not only makes the task less daunting but also provides a sense of accomplishment with each completed step, encouraging you to keep going.

Creating a structured morning routine can be an effective way to fight procrastination. Begin your day with a clear, prioritized plan. Decide on one or two key tasks that you must accomplish in the morning. This clarity serves as a roadmap, guiding your actions and preventing you from wandering off course. Incorporate time-blocking techniques, where you allocate specific time slots for particular tasks. This method helps in maintaining focus and avoiding distractions.

In addition to planning, setting deadlines can act as a powerful motivator. Self-imposed deadlines create a sense of urgency, similar to the pressure of external deadlines. Combine this with rewards for meeting your goals, and you have a solid strategy to overcome procrastination. Rewards can be as simple as taking a short break, enjoying a cup of coffee, or indulging in a favorite activity. This balance of work and reward keeps your motivation levels high.

One effective tactic is the "Two-Minute Rule." If a task takes less than two minutes to complete, do it immediately. This approach prevents small tasks from accumulating and becoming overwhelming. It's surprising how many little tasks we postpone, and how quickly they can pile up. By addressing them right away, you reduce clutter, both physically and mentally, freeing up more time and energy for bigger tasks.

Your environment plays a significant role in either fostering or hindering procrastination. A cluttered workspace can be distracting and overwhelming, making it easier to put off important tasks. Take some time to organize your space, ensuring it's conducive to focus and productivity. Remove any unnecessary items that might distract you and arrange your essentials in a way that promotes efficiency.

Utilize accountability to combat procrastination. Sharing your goals and progress with someone else can create a sense of responsibility. This could be a friend, a colleague, or an online accountability group. Regular check-ins ensure that you stay on track and offer encouragement and support when needed. There's something about knowing someone else is aware of your goals and deadlines that makes you push harder to meet them.

Mindfulness and stress management techniques can also play a crucial role in dealing with procrastination. Practices such as meditation, deep breathing exercises, or even a simple walk can help reduce anxiety and clear your mind. A calm, focused mind is better equipped to tackle tasks efficiently and avoid the trap of procrastination. Taking a few moments to breathe and center yourself can make a significant difference in how you approach your work.

Sometimes, despite our best efforts, procrastination still rears its head. In these moments, practice self-compassion. Berating yourself for procrastinating can lead to a negative cycle of guilt and avoidance. Instead, acknowledge the slip-up and refocus on your goals. Understand that occasional procrastination is human and doesn't define your overall productivity. Building a positive mindset towards overcoming setbacks is essential for long-term success.

Finally, reflect on your progress regularly. Periodic reviews of what you've achieved can provide insight into what's working and what's not. This practice allows you to make necessary adjustments to your morning routine and productivity strategies. Celebrate your successes, no matter how small, and learn from your challenges. Progress is a journey, not a destination, and each step forward is a victory.

By understanding the underlying reasons for procrastination and implementing targeted strategies to counteract it, you can transform your procrastination habits into patterns of productivity and growth. This shift not only enhances your morning routine but also paves the way for sustained success in your personal and professional life.

Battling Morning Fatigue

Morning fatigue can feel like a relentless adversary, particularly for ambitious professionals aiming to kickstart their day with energy and enthusiasm. Waking up groggy and unmotivated can stall productivity and negatively impact one's well-being, making it vital to tackle this challenge with effective strategies.

One crucial factor in combating morning fatigue is establishing a consistent wake-up time. Our bodies thrive on routine, and when we wake up at the same time every day, our internal clock—our circadian rhythm—gets the memo. This alignment can reduce grogginess and help us feel more awake and refreshed. It might be tempting to sleep in on weekends, but maintaining consistency can actually improve overall sleep quality and morning alertness.

Hydration is another key element. After hours of sleep, our bodies often wake up dehydrated, which can exacerbate feelings of fatigue. Drinking a glass of water as soon as you get up can give you an immediate energy boost. Try placing a glass or bottle of water on your nightstand to make this a habit. Even mild dehydration can lead to fatigue, reduced alertness, and decreased cognitive function, so staying hydrated is crucial.

Nutrition can't be overlooked when battling morning fatigue. Consuming a balanced breakfast rich in protein, healthy fats, and complex carbohydrates can provide sustained energy throughout the morning. Foods like nuts, whole grains, fruits, and eggs offer the essential nutrients your body needs to function optimally. Avoid sugary cereals and pastries because they can cause a spike in blood sugar followed by a crash, leaving you more tired than before.

Implementing a morning exercise routine can also significantly diminish feelings of morning fatigue. Physical activity helps increase blood flow and releases endorphins, which act as natural mood lifters. You don't have to run a marathon to feel the benefits—simple stretching or a brisk walk can suffice. These activities can wake up your body and mind, setting a positive tone for the rest of the day.

Getting outside into natural light first thing in the morning can also help reset your circadian rhythms and boost alertness. Sunlight exposure halts the production of melatonin, the sleep hormone, and helps in producing serotonin, the hormone that boosts mood and helps you feel awake. Aim for at least 15 minutes of morning sunlight to reap these benefits.

Mindfulness practices like meditation and deep-breathing exercises can also aid in reducing morning sluggishness. Beginning the day with a clear, focused mind can make it easier to transition into your daily activities. These practices help in lowering cortisol levels in your body, reducing stress, and improving emotional well-being. Even five minutes can make a substantial difference.

Sleep quality the night before is another pivotal aspect. It's not just about the number of hours you sleep but the quality of that sleep. Creating a calming bedtime routine, such as reading or taking a warm bath, can signal to your body that it's time to wind down. Avoiding screens and electronic devices at least an hour before bed can prevent the blue light from interfering with your body's production of melatonin.

For those occasional days when you just didn't get enough sleep, an effective trick is to utilize strategic napping. A short nap of 10-20 minutes can help refresh your alertness and improve cognitive performance without leading to grogginess. Try to nap in the early afternoon so it doesn't interfere with your nighttime sleep.

Caffeine can be a double-edged sword in the battle against morning fatigue. While a cup of coffee can jolt you into wakefulness, relying too much on caffeine can lead to dependency and even disrupt your sleep patterns, creating a vicious cycle. Use it judiciously and consider replacing an afternoon coffee with a more hydrating option like herbal tea.

Developing a positive morning mantra or practicing gratitude can shift your mindset from fatigue to motivation. Take a moment each morning to reflect on what you're grateful for or to set a positive intention for the day. This can create an emotional uplift, giving you the mental energy to overcome physical tiredness.

CHAPTER 20: OVERCOMING COMMON CHALLENGES

Proper time management in the morning can also prevent feelings of fatigue. Rushed mornings create unnecessary stress, sapping your energy reserves before you've even started the day. Prepare as much as possible the night before—lay out your clothes, pack your lunch, and have your to-do list ready. A smooth, organized start can make mornings less daunting and more manageable.

Battling morning fatigue starts with understanding and respecting your body's needs. By incorporating consistent habits, fueling your body with the right nutrients and hydration, and fostering a healthy environment both mentally and physically, you can transform your mornings from sluggish starts to powerful beginnings. Remember, the way you start your morning sets the tone for the rest of the day, making it a vital aspect of your productivity and personal growth journey.

Stay compassionate with yourself during this process. Change doesn't happen overnight, but every small step you take is a progress towards a brighter, more energetic morning. Your commitment to overcoming morning fatigue is not just about fighting tiredness; it's about creating a foundation for a successful, fulfilling day.

Chapter 21: The Importance of Reflection

Amid the hustle and flow of our daily routines, taking a moment for reflection can feel like an unnecessary luxury. Yet, it's precisely these moments of pause that fuel our growth and keep us aligned with our goals. Reflection isn't about ruminating on what's gone by or criticizing every misstep; rather, it's an opportunity to celebrate wins, understand setbacks, and make informed adjustments. End-of-month reviews, for instance, create a structured space to assess what's working and what needs tweaking. Through regular reflection, we cultivate a cycle of continuous improvement, ensuring our morning routines remain effective and responsive to our evolving needs. Embrace these reflective practices, and you'll not only optimize your mornings but also set a foundation for long-term personal and professional growth.

End-of-Month Reviews

Life moves quickly, and without periodic reflection, meaningful growth can easily elude us. This is why end-of-month reviews stand as a crucial practice for anyone looking to maintain a purposeful and effective morning routine. It's during these reviews that you give yourself the opportunity to step back, assess, and realign with your initial goals. So often, the efforts we make every day become a blur, and it's only through regular reflection that we can gain clarity.

Think of your end-of-month review as pressing the 'pause' button. It's a time to ask yourself: "What worked well? What needs adjustment?" The

CHAPTER 21: THE IMPORTANCE OF REFLECTION

answers to these questions can pave the way for more informed decisions moving forward. By taking this moment to engage in introspection, you're not just observing your progress; you're actively shaping your path ahead.

Grab a notebook or open your journal, and dedicate some time—whether it's an hour or even just fifteen minutes—to this practice. Begin with an overview of your month. Revisit the goals you set out at the beginning and see how closely your daily actions aligned with achieving them. This exercise not only helps in identifying patterns but also shows where there is room for improvement.

It's essential to be honest during your reflection. Avoid sugar-coating your performance. If there were days when you faltered, own it. Understanding the 'why' behind these moments can be illuminating. Did you face unexpected obstacles? Were there days when you struggled more than usual? Reflecting on these points can help build strategies to mitigate similar issues in the future.

Conversely, take the time to celebrate your wins, no matter how small they seem. Every step forward counts. Recognizing your achievements, whether it's sticking to a new exercise regimen or finding that perfect morning playlist, is key to maintaining motivation. This balance of constructive critique and celebration fosters a healthy mindset for continuous growth.

A useful method for this review is the SWOT analysis: assessing Strengths, Weaknesses, Opportunities, and Threats. By categorizing your reflections, you can systematically understand different aspects of your month. Strengths highlight what's working well, weaknesses point out areas that need improvement, opportunities identify potential areas for growth and threats outline challenges you may need to prepare for.

Strengths might include aspects of your morning routine that you found most enjoyable or beneficial. Perhaps you discovered that journaling brought you clarity, or maybe those early morning workouts left you feeling energized throughout the day. Knowing what works allows you to double down on these practices.

On the flip side, weaknesses don't mean failure—they indicate what hasn't gone as planned. Maybe you struggled to wake up as early as you intended because your sleep hygiene wasn't ideal. Recognizing this shortfall can guide adjustments in your evening habits to support a better morning routine.

Opportunities are areas ripe for new exploration. If you noticed gaps in your energy levels mid-morning, you might find that introducing a quick stretch or hydration break could make a big difference. Always be on the lookout for tweaks and modifications to keep your routine fresh and effective.

Reflecting on threats involves acknowledging external factors that may be hindering your progress. Perhaps certain obligations or responsibilities disrupted your routine. Identifying these can help you plan around them and develop a more resilient routine. This might mean setting more flexible goals or creating contingency plans.

Another powerful tool for your review is tracking metrics. Quantitative data such as the number of days you met your wake-up time, steps taken, minutes spent meditating, or pages read offer tangible evidence of your progress. This data not only provides concrete proof of your efforts but also helps in identifying trends and making necessary adjustments.

Don't underestimate the emotional aspect of your review. Reflect on how your routine made you feel. Were there specific practices that significantly boosted your mood or stress levels? Emotional wellbeing is an integral part of personal growth and productivity. Acknowledge your feelings and let them guide your routine adjustments.

Your end-of-month review is also an excellent time to revisit your broader life vision and ensure your morning routine aligns with it. Are the habits you're cultivating in the mornings translating to progress in your professional and personal aspirations? If not, consider integrating more targeted practices that support those larger goals.

One more idea is to document any insights or revelations. Writing down these reflections helps solidify your learning and provides a record you can look back on. It's enlightening to see your journey mapped out over several months, offering both a sense of achievement and clarity on recurring issues.

Remember, end-of-month reviews are not about judgment but about awareness and growth. They offer a space for recalibration, ensuring that your efforts are continuously optimized for better results. Making this a ritual helps in maintaining a dynamic and adaptable routine, one that evolves with you.

Moreover, share your findings with accountability partners or communities if you have them. Hearing others' experiences and gaining new perspectives can be incredibly valuable. The exchange of ideas often sparks innovative solutions and strengthens your commitment to your routine.

As you finish your review, set clear, actionable goals for the coming month. These goals should be specific, measurable, achievable, relevant, and time-bound (SMART). This structured goal-setting process ensures that your reflections translate into tangible steps, propelling you forward.

To conclude, making end-of-month reviews a cornerstone of your routine fosters a mindset of continuous improvement. It's through these deliberate pauses for introspection that you'll find the insights necessary to refine your morning practices. Over time, this cycle of reflection and adjustment not only enhances your productivity and wellbeing but also brings you closer to your fullest potential. By committing to this monthly practice, you take control of your growth journey, one morning at a time.

Adjusting for Continuous Improvement

Once you've established a morning routine that works, it's easy to fall into the trap of thinking your work is done. But just like any other aspect of personal growth and productivity, your morning routine should be a living, breathing part of your life. It should evolve as you do. Continuous improvement isn't just a buzzword; it's a critical component in maintaining the efficacy of your routine and ensuring it continues to serve you as your needs and circumstances change.

Reflection is the springboard for this continuous improvement. At the end of each month, when you sit down to review your experiences and assess what is working and what isn't, you gain invaluable insights. This reflection isn't strictly about scrutinizing what went wrong; it's about celebrating what went right, too. A balanced approach helps you understand the intricacies of your daily successes and setbacks, thus allowing you to make informed adjustments.

Begin by asking yourself specific questions: Did your current routine help you achieve your monthly goals? Are there elements that seemed redundant or unproductive? For instance, maybe you consistently found that your morning workout left you too exhausted to focus on work, indicating it might be better shifted to later in the day. On the other hand, perhaps your meditation session noticeably improved your focus and mental clarity, suggesting it should be a permanent fixture.

It's also important to be flexible and open-minded. Variety, after all, is the spice of life. Stagnation can quickly lead to monotony, which can, in turn, lead to decreased motivation. Mixing things up every now and then can keep your morning routine fresh and exciting. Consider experimenting with new activities or altering the order of your existing ones. These small changes can infuse new energy into your routine, making it more enjoyable and effective.

Feedback tends to be more valuable when it's detailed and actionable. Use a journal exclusively dedicated to your morning routines. Document your feelings, experiences, and thoughts. Paying close attention to emotional cues can be particularly insightful. Did a specific part of your routine make you feel particularly motivated or relaxed? Did something trigger stress or anxiety? Understanding the emotional impact of each element in your routine allows you to fine-tune it for maximum personal benefit.

Technology can also be a valuable ally here. Use tracking apps to keep an eye on different aspects of your routine. From sleep quality to physical activity and even meditation effectiveness, these tools can provide quantitative data that complements your qualitative observations. Numbers and statistics often reveal patterns that might not be immediately obvious, providing additional insights into what aspects of your routine need adjustment.

Another dimension to consider is seasonal changes and their impact on your routine. As the seasons change, so do daylight hours, temperature, and even general mood. A winter morning routine might understandably be different from a summer one. Perhaps outdoor activities like running or yoga make more sense during warmer months, while reading or indoor workouts are more appealing during colder months. Adjusting your routine in sync with

CHAPTER 21: THE IMPORTANCE OF REFLECTION

the seasons can keep it balanced and aligned with your natural tendencies and environmental realities.

Getting feedback from others can also be incredibly enlightening. Sharing your morning routine with close friends, family, or even a mentor and asking for their thoughts can provide new perspectives. Sometimes, an external viewpoint can identify blind spots that you didn't notice. They might offer suggestions based on their own experiences, which can be adapted to fit your context.

It's also beneficial to revisit your core goals periodically. What you aimed to achieve at the beginning of the year may evolve as you attain new milestones or face unforeseen challenges. If your goals change, your morning routine should adapt accordingly to support the new objectives. Being clear about what you want to accomplish allows you to tailor your activities specifically toward achieving those aspirations.

Incorporating mindfulness into your routine adjustment process is equally important. Take a few minutes during your reflection periods to simply sit quietly and think about how each element of your routine makes you feel. Mindfulness fosters a deeper awareness and understanding of your day-to-day experiences, empowering you to make more meaningful adjustments.

Remember, continuous improvement doesn't mean constant overhaul. The idea is not to perpetually reinvent your routine but to keep it in a state of steady evolution. Small tweaks and minor adjustments made over time can lead to significant improvements. The goal is to ensure that your morning routine remains an effective tool for enhancing your productivity, wellbeing, and overall growth.

Finally, celebrate your achievements. Acknowledging the progress you've made can be incredibly motivating. It reminds you of the benefits of your efforts and encourages you to keep striving for even better results. Whether it's treating yourself to a small reward or simply taking a moment to appreciate how far you've come, celebrating your successes can provide the emotional boost necessary to keep going.

In the journey of life, each day presents new opportunities and challenges. By continuously refining your morning routine, you ensure that you're prepared to face them head-on, optimized for success and fulfillment. Your morning routine is your launchpad; through reflection and constant adjustment, it can propel you to heights you never thought possible.

Chapter 22: The Long-Term Impact of Morning Routines

The long-term impact of a well-curated morning routine extends far beyond immediate productivity bursts. Studies show that individuals who consistently stick to a structured morning routine experience significant improvements in overall longevity and health. By establishing habits that prioritize physical well-being, mental clarity, and emotional balance, we set a strong foundation for sustained career growth and personal development. This consistent alignment of daily actions with long-term goals cultivates resilience, adaptability, and a mindset geared towards continuous improvement. The ripple effect of such routines often translates into enhanced work performance, better stress management, and richer personal relationships, demonstrating that the real power of morning routines lies in their cumulative benefits over time.

Studies on Longevity and Health

Morning routines aren't just about jumpstarting your day—they can significantly impact your long-term health and longevity. Numerous studies have explored the correlation between consistent morning habits and overall well-being, indicating that how you start your day can set the tone for a healthier, longer life.

One of the key findings in the realm of morning routines and longevity is the association with cardiovascular health. For example, research published in the *Journal of the American College of Cardiology* reveals that individuals who engage in morning exercise routines showed better heart health markers, such as lower blood pressure levels and improved arterial function. These habits also contribute to a reduced risk of heart diseases, a leading cause of mortality worldwide.

Equally compelling are studies focusing on the mental health benefits of structured morning activities. Consistent morning routines have been linked to lower rates of depression and anxiety. According to a study published in *The Lancet Psychiatry*, individuals who maintain regular sleep and wake times have better mental health and emotional stability. This is largely because morning routines often incorporate activities like meditation, journaling, or light exercise, all of which have been shown to reduce stress hormones and increase overall mood.

Another significant area of research is the impact of morning routines on metabolic health. It turns out that starting your day with a healthy breakfast and some form of physical activity can regulate blood sugar levels and improve insulin sensitivity. A study from the *American Journal of Clinical Nutrition* demonstrated that people who consume a balanced breakfast within a couple of hours of waking up have better glucose metabolism throughout the day. This is crucial for preventing metabolic disorders such as type 2 diabetes.

But it doesn't stop there. Studies also show that morning routines can influence longevity through weight management. Engaging in morning exercise, for instance, not only helps in burning calories but also boosts metabolism for the rest of the day. A study published in the *International Journal of Obesity* found that people who exercise in the morning are more likely to stick to their workout plans, leading to sustainable weight loss and reduced obesity-related health risks.

Social connections play a role too. Incorporating social elements into your morning routine, like spending time with family members or participating in a community exercise group, can contribute to a sense of belonging and emotional well-being. Loneliness and social isolation are known risk factors for premature mortality, as noted in a study published in *Public Health*. Building these social interactions into your morning can act as a buffer against

CHAPTER 22: THE LONG-TERM IMPACT OF MORNING ROUTINES

these risks.

Moreover, the consistent practice of mindfulness activities in the morning has been shown to lengthen telomeres, which are the protective caps on the ends of our chromosomes. Shortened telomeres are associated with aging and a higher risk of disease. A study published in *Psychoneuroendocrinology* found that daily mindfulness practices could maintain telomere length, potentially extending lifespan.

Furthermore, sticking to a regular morning routine can enhance sleep quality, which is directly linked to longevity. Poor sleep has been associated with numerous chronic health issues, including hypertension, obesity, and cardiovascular disease. By maintaining a consistent wake-up time, you help regulate your body's internal clock, leading to more restful and restorative sleep. Research published in *SLEEP* journal indicated that individuals with a consistent morning routine had fewer sleep disturbances and experienced better sleep quality, which is crucial for long-term health.

A pivotal study in the *British Medical Journal* explored the health outcomes of early risers versus night owls. The research highlighted that early risers tend to have healthier lifestyle choices and lower incidences of chronic diseases. This could be attributed to the structured nature of their mornings, which often encompasses exercise, nutritious breakfasts, and mental preparation for the day.

On the nutritional front, the habit of morning hydration and balanced breakfasts doesn't just fuel the day's productivity but also impacts long-term health. Hydration is essential for metabolic processes, and a well-rounded breakfast can provide the necessary nutrients to sustain energy levels and maintain metabolic health. A study in the *Journal of Nutrition* correlates regular breakfast consumption with a reduced risk of developing cardiovascular diseases and improved overall nutritional profiles.

Though we've touched on physical health, we must not forget the cognitive benefits linked to morning routines. Activities like reading, puzzle-solving, or engaging with educational materials can boost brain health. According to a study in *Neuroscience Research*, engaging in intellectually stimulating activities in the morning can enhance cognitive functions like memory, attention, and problem-solving, which could contribute to cognitive health in later years.

In summary, the evidence supporting the long-term benefits of morning routines is overwhelming. By selecting and consistently practicing activities that enhance physical, mental, and emotional health, you're investing in your longevity. Morning routines act as the foundation for a healthier, more balanced lifestyle, offering a myriad of benefits that extend well beyond immediate productivity and satisfaction.

Whether it's a brisk morning walk, a mindful meditation session, or simply taking the time to eat a nutritious breakfast, each small step taken in the morning compounds into significant health benefits over time. By implementing and sticking to a well-structured morning routine, you're not only setting yourself up for daily success but also paving the way for a longer, healthier life.

Career and Personal Growth

Adopting a consistent and purposeful morning routine goes beyond enhancing your immediate productivity; it sets a foundation for long-term career and personal growth. When you start your day with intention and focus, you're essentially programming yourself for success, not just for the day, but for the months and years ahead.

In the world of ambitious professionals, mornings are golden. Starting early gives you a head start on the day, allowing you to tackle high-priority tasks before the rest of the world wakes up. Over time, this edge compounds, leading to greater efficiency and achievement in your career.

Your morning routine can serve as a mini-trial run of sorts, preparing you for the day's challenges. Whether you're an entrepreneur, a corporate heavyweight, or an artist, the discipline of consistency and routine equips you with a toolkit that can handle various scenarios. You're cultivating a habit of preparedness.

Imagine having a ritual that includes goal-setting and mental rehearsal for the day ahead. Visualization and positive affirmations, for example, help you to mentally navigate through your day's challenges even before you've had your first cup of coffee. By the time you arrive at work, meetings, or creative tasks, you're already in the right mindset to succeed.

Moreover, personal growth is inherently linked to the routines we cultivate. Journaling, for instance, isn't just a record of daily events but a mirror reflecting your progress and areas where growth is needed. When you note down your experiences and thoughts, you create a feedback loop that drives continuous personal development.

Let's talk about learning and skill-building, a vital aspect of both personal and career growth. Your morning time can be an oasis for reading, engaging in online courses, or practicing new skills. Even 20-30 minutes each morning can accrue significant knowledge, making you a more rounded and informed individual over time.

Reading thought-provoking material or listening to an educational podcast can inspire new ideas and perspectives. These activities not only make you more knowledgeable but also more creative and innovative in your professional life. An informed and broad-minded individual is often a more effective problem-solver and leader.

A well-structured morning routine also emphasizes the importance of physical well-being, which directly correlates with career performance. Regular exercise boosts your energy levels, reduces stress, and improves cognitive function. It's no coincidence that many high achievers prioritize fitness; it's a crucial component of their success blueprint.

Morning workouts are not just about building muscles; they're about building mental resilience and discipline. The endorphins released during exercise can uplift your mood, making you more optimistic and motivated to tackle the tasks ahead. A healthier body supports a sharper mind, leading to enhanced productivity and decision-making capabilities.

Hydration and a balanced breakfast are often overlooked but are essential. Proper nutrition fuels your body and mind, ensuring you operate at peak efficiency. Imagine a morning routine that starts with a glass of water, a nutritious meal, and perhaps a supplement tailored to your needs. These small habits contribute to sustained energy throughout the day.

Consistency in these practices strengthens your ability to handle stress and adversity. When you face obstacles, your established routines become anchors that keep you grounded. This resilience is vital for career progression and personal growth; it's the ability to bounce back and keep moving forward.

On a broader scale, a robust morning routine cultivates a mindset of proactive rather than reactive behavior. By taking control of your mornings, you shift from merely responding to the day's demands to actively shaping your daily outcomes. This shift in mindset can lead to enhanced leadership qualities and greater fulfillment in both personal and professional life.

In the long run, these morning practices accumulate into significant personal transformation. You become more disciplined, focused, and aligned with your goals. The benefits spill over into every aspect of your life, from work to relationships, and even your sense of self-worth and accomplishment.

In summary, the ripple effects of a well-orchestrated morning routine are profound. They create a structure that fosters career advancement and personal growth, equipping you with the tools and mindset needed to navigate life's challenges successfully. Over time, these small, daily practices can lead to monumental changes in your professional trajectory and personal wellbeing.

Chapter 23: Creating a Morning Routine Community

One of the keys to sustaining a successful morning routine lies in the power of community. Finding accountability partners who share similar goals can provide the motivation and consistency needed to transform habits. Whether it's joining online groups and forums or engaging with local communities, the collective energy and shared experiences can drive you toward greater personal growth. When you connect with others on the same journey, you can exchange best practices, offer encouragement, and celebrate each other's successes. It's about building a network where everyone can thrive, finding the right support system to ensure your morning routine becomes a cornerstone of your daily life.

Finding Accountability Partners

Establishing a morning routine is a transformative journey, but doing it alone can sometimes be challenging. That's where accountability partners come in. These are like-minded individuals who share similar goals and are committed to holding each other accountable. Finding the right accountability partner can be a game-changer in maintaining consistent and effective morning routines.

Imagine waking up to a message from someone who genuinely cares about your progress. This sense of shared purpose creates a powerful incentive to stay on track. Accountability partners provide motivation and support, especially on days when you're tempted to hit the snooze button. Knowing that someone is counting on you makes it that much harder to give in to complacency.

Start by identifying potential partners within your circle of influence. Look for friends, family members, or colleagues who are also interested in enhancing their productivity and well-being. It's essential to find someone whose goals align with yours and who is equally committed to the process. This mutual commitment ensures that both parties are equally invested in each other's success.

Once you've identified a potential partner, have an open and honest conversation about your intentions and expectations. Discuss what you hope to achieve, the challenges you anticipate, and how you can support each other. Creating a shared vision and setting clear boundaries will foster a strong partnership rooted in trust and accountability.

It's also crucial to establish a communication plan with your accountability partner. Decide on the frequency and mode of your check-ins — whether it's daily texts, weekly calls, or in-person meetings. Consistency in communication is key to maintaining momentum and ensuring that both parties remain engaged in the process. Regular updates provide opportunities to celebrate small victories, address setbacks, and recalibrate strategies as needed.

An effective method for fostering accountability is setting joint goals. Shared objectives create a sense of camaraderie and collective responsibility. For instance, you might agree to complete a specific number of morning workouts together virtually or commit to journaling at the same time each day. These joint goals can make the process more enjoyable and less isolating.

Another benefit of having an accountability partner is the opportunity for constructive feedback. Often, we need an outside perspective to identify blind spots or areas where we might be falling short. A good accountability partner provides honest and supportive feedback, helping you stay aligned with your objectives. This feedback loop is invaluable for continuous self-improvement and personal growth.

Consider the emotional and mental support value your accountability partner can provide. Life is full of unexpected challenges, and having someone

CHAPTER 23: CREATING A MORNING ROUTINE COMMUNITY

to lean on during tough times can make a significant difference. They can offer encouragement, remind you of your why, and help you navigate obstacles without losing sight of your goals.

If you can't find someone within your immediate circle, don't worry — there are plenty of other options. Social media and online communities are excellent platforms for finding accountability partners. Websites, forums, and groups dedicated to personal development and productivity are filled with individuals seeking similar connections. The benefit of these virtual partnerships is the diversity of perspectives and experiences, enriching your journey with broader insights.

In today's digital age, various apps and tools facilitate accountability partnerships. Platforms like Habitica, Coach.me, and Strides offer features that allow you to track progress, set reminders, and connect with accountability partners. Utilizing technology can streamline the process and make it easier to stay connected, no matter where you are.

But remember, the essence of an accountability partnership goes beyond just mechanical check-ins or digital updates. It's about forming a meaningful connection with someone who genuinely cares about your success and well-being. Investing time, energy, and sincerity into these relationships will pay off manifold in your journey toward cultivating a consistent and effective morning routine.

By being an accountability partner yourself, you also reap the benefits of the partnership. Supporting someone else's journey helps reinforce your commitment and deepens your understanding of the process. Teaching and guiding others can solidify your practices and inspire continuous self-reflection and growth.

In essence, finding the right accountability partner blends the best of shared experience, mutual encouragement, and the pursuit of common goals. It's about building a supportive community, even if that community is just one other person. This connection can elevate your morning routine from a solitary endeavor to a shared mission filled with motivation, inspiration, and sustained progress. So, take the initiative to find the right partner. Your future self will thank you.

Joining Online Groups and Forums

While creating a morning routine community is about fostering accountability and mutual support, a significant part of this journey involves extending that community into online spaces. Joining online groups and forums can offer a wealth of advantages, providing a platform where you can share progress, seek advice, and feel consistently inspired. This section dives deep into how you can effectively engage with these digital communities and make the most out of the resources they offer.

First and foremost, online groups and forums offer an unmatched variety of perspectives. In these communities, you'll find members from different walks of life, each bringing in their unique take on morning routines. This diversity can provide fresh insights and innovative ideas you may not have considered. Plus, seeing how others overcome challenges similar to yours can be incredibly motivating. It's reassuring to know you're not alone in your quest for self-improvement.

Finding the right group can start with simple searches on platforms like Facebook, Reddit, and specialized forums like those on wellness websites. Facebook, for instance, has numerous groups geared toward various aspects of morning routines—from planning and organization to specific activities like meditation or workouts. Reddit is another treasure trove, where subreddits dedicated to productivity, mindfulness, and personal development thrive. A simple search can lead you to communities with thousands of members ready to share their experiences.

However, it's not just about joining any group; it's about finding the right fit for you. Spend some time lurking—observe the conversation dynamics, the types of content shared, and the overall tone of the community. Are discussions constructive and encouraging? Are the members' goals and struggles similar to yours? Focus on quality over quantity when it comes to choosing your groups. A smaller, more engaged community can often be more beneficial than a larger one where your voice gets lost in the crowd.

Once you've identified the right groups, it's essential to actively participate. Lurking can give you an idea of the community's vibe but contributing is how you build connections. Share your milestones and challenges, and don't hesitate to ask for advice. It's through these interactions that you'll form relationships and foster mutual accountability. In turn, you'll find that being in a supportive environment will amplify your own commitment to your morning routine.

Moreover, online groups are great for tapping into collective wisdom. For example, if you're struggling with consistently waking up early, you might find practical tips shared by long-time members. Some might suggest using specific alarm apps that gradually wake you up with natural sounds, while others may swear by going to bed and waking up at the same time every day, including weekends.

Online forums and groups can also be a crucible for experimentation. These are spaces where new methods and tools are shared almost daily. Maybe someone is trying out a new meditation app or a unique workout routine, and they share their experience. You can learn from their trial and error, thereby saving yourself time and effort. This sense of collective learning is invaluable for anyone serious about refining their morning routine.

Another key advantage of online groups is the exposure to accountability structures that might not exist in your offline life. Many groups organize weekly or monthly challenges, goal-setting sessions, and check-ins. Engaging in these activities keeps you accountable to not just yourself but to the community at large. Celebrating your wins with the group and getting cheered on can provide a significant morale boost.

Frequently, these communities will provide access to resources that can aid in your personal growth journey. This could range from book recommendations to webinars led by experts in productivity and wellbeing. Some forums even have file sections where members upload templates, planners, and other tools that have been particularly useful for them. These resources can be handy for structuring your routine more effectively.

To make the most out of these online communities, it's also critical to balance consumption with action. It's easy to spend hours reading tips and stories, but real progress happens when you apply what you've learned. Consider setting boundaries around how much time you spend in these groups.

Use that time to engage purposefully rather than passively scrolling through posts.

Ultimately, the relationships cultivated in these groups can extend beyond the virtual realm. Many online communities organize meetups or events where members can connect in person. Such gatherings can deepen the bonds formed online and provide a new layer of accountability and support. If you ever get the chance to attend one of these meetups, take it. The in-person connection can reinforce and invigorate your commitment to your morning routine.

Integrating yourself into an online community dedicated to morning routines is more than just another trick to boost productivity—it's about becoming part of a supportive network that drives continual improvement. Leveraging the power of collective wisdom, varied perspectives, and accountability can significantly enhance your journey toward creating a morning routine that sets you up for success. So, explore these online spaces, actively participate, and let the community help you to elevate your morning routine to new heights.

Chapter 24: Custom Routines for Specific Goals

When it comes to crafting a morning routine that propels you toward your specific goals, customization is key. Entrepreneurs might prioritize quiet time for strategic thinking and setting business priorities, which can include activities like meditation and planning. On the other hand, students may find more benefit in dedicating morning hours to revision and exercise to boost cognitive function. Creating a personalized routine means carefully evaluating what activities align with your aspirations and daily challenges. Tailoring your morning practices this way ensures that each element of your routine serves a purpose, fueling your progress and setting a powerful tone for the rest of your day.

Routines for Entrepreneurs

Entrepreneurs are a breed apart, driven by ambition, innovation, and an unyielding desire to make things happen. In a world where every minute counts, crafting a morning routine that maximizes productivity and nurtures well-being is essential. The morning hours serve as a launchpad, setting the tone for the day ahead. For entrepreneurs, this period is not just about ticking off tasks but about creating a mindset geared towards success and sustainability.

Start with Clarity

One of the first tasks for any entrepreneur's morning routine is achieving mental clarity. This often begins with a few minutes of meditation or deep-breathing exercises. Practicing mindfulness helps center your thoughts and prepares your mind for the challenges ahead. It's in these quiet moments that you can set clear intentions and goals for the day. If meditation isn't your thing, try a few minutes of reflective journaling. Writing down your thoughts, worries, and objectives can work wonders in unburdening your mind and providing a clear roadmap for the day.

Set Priorities

Entrepreneurs often juggle numerous responsibilities. This is why setting priorities is crucial. A useful technique is the "Rule of Three." At the start of your day, list the top three tasks that will move your business forward. These aren't just any tasks. They should be high-impact activities aligned with your long-term objectives. By concentrating on just three primary goals, you make your day less overwhelming and more productive. As the great Peter Drucker said, "Efficiency is doing things right; effectiveness is doing the right things."

Morning Movement

Physical activity is another cornerstone of a successful entrepreneur's morning routine. Exercise fuels both your body and your brain, giving you the energy and mental clarity needed to tackle complex problems. Whether it's a quick jog, a session at the gym, or some morning yoga, movement invigorates your body and mind. Many successful entrepreneurs swear by their morning workouts as essential components of their daily rituals. Exercise not only improves physical health but also reduces stress and anxiety, enhancing your ability to make sound decisions.

Fuel Your Body

Nutrition plays a vital role in sustaining the demanding lifestyle of an entrepreneur. A balanced breakfast can set the stage for a day full of energy and focus. Opt for meals rich in protein, healthy fats, and fiber to keep you satiated and mentally sharp. Skipping breakfast or consuming sugary snacks can lead to energy crashes, making it harder to maintain productivity. Preparing a nutritious breakfast shouldn't be complicated. Simple options like a smoothie packed with fruits, vegetables, and protein can provide the

CHAPTER 24: CUSTOM ROUTINES FOR SPECIFIC GOALS

energy you need without consuming too much time.

Continuous Learning

For entrepreneurs, personal development is an ongoing journey. Mornings are an excellent time to invest in learning and skill-building. This could mean reading a book, listening to a business podcast, or even taking an online course. Dedicating just 20-30 minutes each morning to learning something new can accumulate over time, providing valuable insights and a competitive edge in your industry. Remember, the most successful entrepreneurs are those who never stop learning.

Networking and Connection

Although mornings might seem like a solitary time, it's also an ideal moment for connecting with key people. Whether it's sending a quick email to a mentor, touching base with a business partner, or planning your social media strategy, these small but meaningful interactions can lay the groundwork for fruitful relationships. Building and maintaining a strong network is essential for growth and can provide invaluable support and insight.

Visualize Success

Many entrepreneurs practice visualization to start their day. Before diving into the hustle, take a few minutes to visualize your success. Imagine the steps you'll take throughout the day, the meetings you have planned, and the challenges you'll overcome. Visualization reinforces a positive mindset and builds confidence in achieving your goals. The simple act of mentally rehearsing your day can make a substantial difference in how you perform.

Strategic Planning

Effective strategic planning can often be the difference between a day well spent and a day wasted. Utilize morning time to outline your major projects and break them down into manageable tasks. A well-thought-out plan not only keeps you on track but also enables you to make adjustments as needed. Many successful entrepreneurs use planning tools and apps to help with this, ensuring they stay organized and focused.

End on an Energizing Note

Conclude your morning routine with an energizing ritual. This could be something as simple as a cold shower, a short burst of physical exercise, or listening to an uplifting song. The idea is to end your morning routine feeling energized and ready to tackle the day's challenges. The importance of positive energy cannot be overstated, as it significantly impacts your outlook and performance.

Final Thoughts

Crafting a morning routine tailored for entrepreneurial success is not just about mimicking what others do. It's about finding what works best for you. Experiment with different activities, track their impact, and refine your routine until it becomes a powerful tool for productivity and personal growth. As with any habit, consistency is key. The more you stick to your routine, the more natural it will become, eventually turning into an integral part of your daily life.

To sum up, a successful morning routine for entrepreneurs is one that balances mental clarity, strategic planning, physical activity, and continuous learning. It's about setting priorities, fueling the body, and creating energizing rituals. By dedicating the first hours of your day to these activities, you set yourself up for a day of heightened productivity, creativity, and success.

Routines for Students

For students, morning routines can be transformational, creating a foundation that not only enhances academic performance but also fosters a balanced and fulfilling life. The demands on students are unique and often multifaceted, ranging from academic pressures and extracurricular activities to the ever-evolving social dynamics. With so much on their plates, structuring a morning routine that addresses these specific needs can significantly boost productivity, mental clarity, and overall well-being.

The first step in crafting the ideal morning routine is setting a realistic wake-up time. For most students, the morning can feel like a rush against the clock, primarily because they may not be getting enough sleep. Establishing a consistent wake-up time that allows for sufficient rest and a calm start to the day can make a world of difference. While it might be tempting to hit the

CHAPTER 24: CUSTOM ROUTINES FOR SPECIFIC GOALS

snooze button, the scientifically-backed benefits of waking up early—such as improved cognitive function and emotional stability—are too compelling to ignore.

Once awake, hydration should be at the top of the list. Drinking a glass of water as soon as you get out of bed helps kickstart your metabolism and aids in detoxifying your system. Given that the brain is 75% water, staying hydrated can enhance focus and cognitive performance, which is crucial for tackling a demanding school day.

Moving on, a balanced breakfast is essential. Skipping breakfast or opting for sugary cereals can lead to a spike and subsequent dip in blood sugar levels, affecting concentration and energy. Instead, prioritize meals rich in protein, healthy fats, and complex carbohydrates. Foods like eggs, oatmeal, or a smoothie with fruits and vegetables can provide sustained energy and keep you full until lunchtime.

Incorporating some form of physical activity in the morning, even if it's just a 10-minute stretch, can have significant benefits. Exercise releases endorphins, which improve mood and enhance concentration. It doesn't have to be an intense workout; simple yoga poses or a quick walk can help shake off morning grogginess and prepare both the mind and body for the day ahead. If time permits, engaging in a more structured workout can be even more advantageous.

Students can also benefit immensely from mindfulness practices such as meditation. Taking a few minutes to center oneself can reduce anxiety and improve focus. Practices like deep-breathing exercises, mindfulness meditation, or even a quick gratitude journal entry can set a positive tone for the day, helping students navigate stress and academic challenges with greater ease.

After physical and mindfulness activities, it might be a good idea to engage in some light academic review. This isn't about diving into complex problems but rather a quick, focused review of your day's subjects. Spending just 10-15 minutes skimming through notes or summaries can help cement previously learned material and prepare your brain for the day's upcoming lessons.

Organizing your materials the night before can save valuable time in the morning. Make sure your backpack is packed with necessary books, notebooks, and supplies. This simple act can prevent morning chaos and ensure you're mentally prepared for the day. A clutter-free space leads to a clutter-free mind, making you more open and ready for learning.

Effective planning is another cornerstone of a successful morning routine for students. Take a few moments to review your schedule, set priorities, and outline your tasks for the day. Whether you use a traditional planner, a digital app, or even sticky notes, having a clear plan helps manage time more effectively and reduce stress. It also allows you to set realistic goals and track your progress throughout the day.

In addition to planning, setting daily intentions or affirmations can be incredibly powerful. Statements like "I am capable," "I will stay focused," or "I approach challenges with a positive mindset" can frame your day in a constructive way. These affirmations can help boost confidence and serve as a mental anchor when stress levels rise.

Morning routines can also be an opportunity for personal development. Allocating time for activities like reading or listening to educational podcasts can be a great way to stimulate your mind before heading to class. Whether you're diving into a book related to your studies or exploring new topics for fun, this habit can cultivate a lifelong love for learning.

Finally, social connection shouldn't be overlooked. While mornings are typically seen as a more solitary or family-time moment, taking a brief moment to connect with friends, whether through a quick text or a few minutes chatting over breakfast, can provide emotional support and set a positive emotional tone for the day.

Consistency is key for students when it comes to routines. Building and sticking to a morning routine requires discipline and a bit of trial and error. However, the rewards in terms of improved academic performance, emotional stability, and overall well-being make it well worth the effort. Set small, manageable goals and gradually incorporate these elements into your mornings. Over time, these habits will become second nature, paving the way for success both in and out of the classroom.

In sum, a well-structured morning routine tailored to the unique needs of

CHAPTER 24: CUSTOM ROUTINES FOR SPECIFIC GOALS

students can provide the tools needed for academic and personal success. By focusing on hydration, nutrition, physical activity, mindfulness, organization, planning, and personal development, students can create a balanced and empowering start to their day. This methodology not only enhances productivity and focus but also contributes to a more joyful and less stressful school experience.

Chapter 25: Reinforcing Your Routine with Evening Habits

As the sun dips and your day draws to a close, the evening provides a powerful opportunity to set the stage for tomorrow's success. Reinforcing your morning routine requires mindful evening habits that prepare your mind and body for rest and rejuvenation. Start by developing a consistent wind-down schedule that includes activities like reading, light stretching, or practicing gratitude. Disconnect from screens at least an hour before bed to allow your brain to transition smoothly into sleep mode. Lay out your clothes, plan your breakfast, and jot down the next day's priorities; these simple actions can dissolve morning chaos and foster a sense of readiness. By cultivating these evening rituals, you align your environment and mindset, paving the way for a more productive and peaceful start to each day.

Preparing the Night Before

Success doesn't happen by accident; it's often the result of deliberate actions and choices made ahead of time. When we talk about building a productive morning routine, the groundwork truly begins the night before. By taking specific, mindful actions in the evening, you set the stage for a morning that fosters productivity and wellbeing.

First, let's consider the environment where you'll be starting your day. A clutter-free space can significantly impact your mental clarity and focus. Spend a few minutes tidying up your workspace or living area each evening.

CHAPTER 25: REINFORCING YOUR ROUTINE WITH EVENING HABITS

Remove unnecessary items from your desk, lay out any documents or tools you'll need for the following day, and ensure that everything is in its rightful place. This simple practice can save you from morning chaos and allow you to dive straight into your tasks with a clear mind.

Equally important is planning your outfit. Deciding what to wear in the morning can be surprisingly time-consuming and mentally draining. Choose your clothes the night before and lay them out neatly. This will not only save you precious minutes in the morning but also reduce decision fatigue, allowing you to reserve your mental energy for more important tasks.

When it comes to nutrition, preparing a portion of your breakfast the night before can be a game-changer. Consider making overnight oats, preparing smoothie ingredients, or even setting up a coffee maker to start brewing at a specific time. Having these elements ready to go ensures that you'll start your day with a nutritious meal, without the need to rush or make impulsive, less healthy choices.

Planning your day the night before is essential. Take some time in the evening to review your schedule and set your priorities. Write down your top three to five tasks that need your attention the next day. This not only helps you wake up with a clear sense of direction but also reduces morning stress. You'll know exactly what needs to be tackled, aligning your actions with your larger goals.

Preparation extends to your mental state as well. Engage in activities that promote relaxation and help you unwind. Reading a book, journaling, or practicing mindfulness can create a serene transition between a busy day and a restful night. Journaling is particularly effective. Recording your thoughts, accomplishments, and even any anxieties you may have can clear your mind, making it easier to fall asleep and wake up refreshed.

Consistency is key, but so is flexibility. If something unexpected comes up in the evening, don't stress about skipping a night of preparation. The goal is to create habits that support you, not to add extra pressure. When you miss a night, simply get back on track the next evening. This resilience will ensure that your routines serve you over the long term, adapting to your lifestyle rather than becoming a rigid set of rules.

Don't underestimate the value of a solid evening routine in fostering quality sleep. Good sleep hygiene is closely connected to how you wind down. Maintain a consistent sleep schedule by going to bed and waking up at the same time every day, even on weekends. This consistency reinforces your body's natural circadian rhythms, improving overall sleep quality and making it easier to wake up feeling refreshed.

Blue light from screens can interfere with your ability to fall asleep, so consider a digital curfew in the hour before bed. Turn off electronics or switch to 'night mode' settings on your devices to minimize exposure to blue light. Instead, use this time to engage in low-stimulation activities like reading, light stretching, or listening to calming music. These practices can signal to your body that it's time to wind down, promoting more restful sleep.

Consider creating a bedtime ritual to signify the end of the day. This could include skincare routines, dimming the lights, or even sipping on a warm herbal tea. Such rituals can create Pavlovian associations in your brain, triggering a relaxation response that prepares you for sleep. Repetition of these actions trains your mind and body to recognize when it's time to transition from wakefulness to rest.

Part of preparing the night before includes minimizing morning friction. If you frequently struggle to find your keys or wallet in the morning, establish a designated spot for essential items like these. Whether it's a small tray by the door or a specific drawer, having a consistent place for your belongings can drastically reduce morning stress and streamline your departure from the house.

Also worth addressing is the temptation to stay up late. This can arise from a variety of factors, such as wanting to finish a captivating show, scrolling through social media, or working late into the night. Recognize these triggers and set boundaries for yourself. If needed, use tools like screen time limits or alarms set 30 minutes before your intended bedtime to remind you to start wrapping up your activities.

Reflecting on your day is another powerful practice. Take a moment to acknowledge what went well and what could be improved. This reflection can help you make better choices and set stronger intentions for the following

CHAPTER 25: REINFORCING YOUR ROUTINE WITH EVENING HABITS

day. Whether it's a quick mental review or a more formal journaling session, ending your day with reflection can provide insights that drive continuous improvement in your routines.

Moreover, considering the emotional aspect of your evening routine can be profoundly impactful. Engage in activities that bring you joy and relaxation. This could involve a hobby, spending time with loved ones, or simply taking a quiet moment for yourself. Cultivating positive emotions before bedtime can lead to a more positive outlook when you wake up, ready to conquer the day.

Integrating these evening habits into your daily routine doesn't have to be overwhelming. Start small and build upon each element gradually. Maybe you begin with laying out your clothes, then add meal prep, and eventually incorporate journaling or meditation. The key is to find what works best for you and adapt these suggestions to your lifestyle. With time and consistency, these practices will become second nature, seamlessly contributing to the efficacy of your morning routine.

Finally, always remember the power of perseverance. Forming new habits takes time, patience, and a willingness to adapt. Some evenings you'll stick to your plan flawlessly; other times, life will throw a curveball. What matters most is your commitment to getting back on track and continuously striving for improvement. Your evening routine is a vital component of your overall success strategy, setting the stage for mornings where you're at your best.

In conclusion, preparing the night before is an investment in your next day's success. It's about creating conditions that support your ambitions and align with your goals. From organizing your environment and planning your day to fostering relaxation and ensuring quality sleep, these actions form the bedrock of an effective morning routine. Start implementing these habits tonight, and feel the difference they make when the morning arrives.

Unwinding Techniques

Setting the stage for a productive morning begins the night before. Evening routines are crucial for winding down and ensuring you get the restorative sleep needed to tackle the day ahead. Unwinding techniques serve as a bridge between your busy day and a peaceful night, creating an essential buffer that separates your active mind from the tranquility needed for deep sleep.

One of the most effective techniques for unwinding is to establish a consistent bedtime. Consistency in sleep patterns can significantly impact your circadian rhythms, allowing your body to optimize rest and recovery. Aim to go to bed and wake up at the same time every day, even on weekends. This consistency helps regulate your internal clock, making it easier to fall asleep and wake up naturally.

Creating a calming bedtime ritual is another powerful unwinding technique. This could include activities such as reading a book, listening to soothing music, or practicing gentle stretches. Avoid activities that are too stimulating, like engaging in intense exercise or consuming caffeine, especially in the hours leading up to bedtime. Soft lighting, calming scents like lavender, and a comfortable sleeping environment can all contribute to a sense of relaxation.

Avoiding screens before bed is crucial in our digital age. The blue light emitted from phones, tablets, and computers can suppress the production of melatonin, a hormone that regulates sleep. Try to disconnect from electronic devices at least an hour before bed. Instead, opt for activities that promote relaxation, such as journaling or meditating. These practices not only calm the mind but also provide an opportunity for reflection and mental clarity.

Engaging in mindfulness or meditation practices can significantly enhance your ability to unwind. Basic breathing exercises, guided meditations, or progressive muscle relaxation can help reduce stress and promote a sense of calm. Mindfulness focuses on staying present and acknowledging your thoughts without judgment, which can ease mental clutter and prepare you for restful sleep.

Incorporating a gratitude practice into your evening routine can also be a profound way to unwind. Taking a few minutes to reflect on the positive aspects of your day helps shift your focus from any stress or negativity you might be carrying. This positive mental state can make it easier to let go of worries and anxieties, laying the groundwork for tranquil sleep.

Nutrition plays a role in how well you unwind, too. A light snack that combines protein and carbohydrates, such as a small piece of cheese with

CHAPTER 25: REINFORCING YOUR ROUTINE WITH EVENING HABITS

whole-grain crackers, can keep your blood sugar stable and help you relax. Avoid heavy, spicy, or sugary foods late in the evening as they can cause discomfort or disrupt sleep.

Developing a pre-sleep routine that works for you takes some experimentation. Some people find a warm bath incredibly soothing, while others may benefit from gentle yoga or stretching. The key is to find activities that help you feel relaxed and ready for sleep. Listening to calming audiobooks or podcasts can also be an effective way to transition from the high-energy demands of the day to a more restful state.

Environmental factors can significantly impact your ability to unwind. Your bedroom should be a sanctuary for sleep. Lower the temperature and consider using blackout curtains to make the room as dark as possible. White noise machines or apps can drown out disruptive sounds, creating a more peaceful environment. Ensuring your mattress and pillows are comfortable and supportive can also make a big difference.

Keeping a consistent evening routine aligns with the broader principle of habit formation. Just as with your morning routine, the consistency you build in the evening creates a night-time rhythm that signals to your body it's time to wind down. Over time, these signals become ingrained, making it easier to fall asleep and wake up refreshed.

Another unwinding technique is to manage your time effectively throughout the day. This means setting boundaries around your work and leisure activities to ensure that your evenings are free from unfinished tasks or lingering stress. When you create clear lines between work time and downtime, it becomes easier to transition into your evening routine.

Reflect on your day with intention. Spend a few minutes acknowledging what went well and what could be improved. This doesn't mean dwelling on mistakes but rather noting them and preparing a plan for the next day. This kind of reflection can free your mind from unresolved worries, allowing you to enter a state of relaxation more smoothly.

Focus on the sensory aspects of your evening routine. Engage your senses with calming elements like a warm cup of herbal tea, the soft glow of dimmed lights, or the comforting texture of your favorite blanket. These tactile experiences can help ground you in the present moment, pushing away the stressors of the day.

Avoid heavy mental activities before bed. While it might be tempting to catch up on work or plan your next day in detail, these activities can activate your mind in ways that make it harder to fall asleep. Instead, leave any detailed planning for the morning or earlier in the evening, ensuring your mind is as restful as your body come bedtime.

Exploring aromatherapy can also be a helpful unwinding technique. Essential oils like lavender, chamomile, and bergamot have calming properties that can reduce stress and promote relaxation. A few drops in a diffuser or sprinkled on your pillow might be all you need to help your mind and body prepare for sleep.

Another aspect to consider is the power of visualization. Before bed, take a few moments to imagine a peaceful and happy place. This could be a beach, a mountain retreat, or even a moment in time when you felt completely at ease. Visualization can help shift your mindset from worry to calm, making it easier to drift off to sleep.

Use the time before bed to connect with loved ones. Whether it's a quick chat with a friend or a cuddle with a pet, human connection can significantly reduce stress and provide a sense of comfort and love. This emotional support can be just what you need to end the day on a positive note.

Incorporating these unwinding techniques into your evening routine can create a foundation for a night of deep, restorative sleep. Sleep, in turn, powers your productivity, creativity, and well-being for the next day. By prioritizing these practices, you're taking deliberate steps to enhance your overall quality of life, ensuring that you're not just ready to tackle the next morning, but every day that follows.

Ultimately, the key to effectively unwinding is to be consistent and intentional with your evening habits. Much like your morning routine sets the tone for the day, your evening routine sets the stage for a rejuvenating night's sleep. Both work harmoniously to bolster your daily productivity and long-term personal growth, creating a virtuous cycle of well-being and success.

Conclusion

The journey toward creating a perfect morning routine is as unique as the individuals who embark on it. From understanding the science behind our circadian rhythms to grasping the benefits of morning productivity, you've explored a comprehensive landscape of strategies and insights designed to elevate your daily life. This book has aimed to empower you with the tools and knowledge necessary to craft and maintain a morning routine that nurtures both your productivity and overall well-being.

What stands out is the power of consistency. By showing up each day and adhering to your carefully designed routine, you build habits that foster resilience, focus, and long-term success. Overcoming obstacles becomes manageable when you treat every hurdle as an opportunity for growth. Consistency isn't about perfection—it's about progress. Even small, incremental steps have a cumulative impact over time.

Your mornings set the tone for the rest of the day. Emphasizing the importance of proper nutrition and hydration in the morning cannot be overstated. A balanced breakfast boosts your energy levels and mental clarity, setting a strong foundation for the day ahead. Hydrating effectively keeps you refreshed and focused, helping you maintain productivity and mental sharpness.

Movement also plays a critical role in your morning routine. Whether it's an invigorating workout, a gentle stretching session, or a few moments of mindfulness through yoga, physical activity primes your body and mind for the day's challenges. It's not about the length or intensity of the exercise but about the consistency and the commitment to maintaining a routine that energizes you.

Equally crucial is tending to your mental and emotional well-being. Practices like meditation and journaling offer a quiet space for reflection, helping you start the day with a clear, focused mind. These moments are invaluable for cultivating emotional resilience and mental clarity.

Planning your day and setting intentions in the morning can offer a sense of direction and control. Crafting a clear plan helps you prioritize tasks and allocate your time effectively. Coupled with positive affirmations, these practices keep you motivated and aligned with your personal and professional goals.

Building a routine around personal development is key to long-term growth. By dedicating morning time to activities like reading, learning new skills, or listening to audiobooks, you invest in your continuous development. This habit not only broadens your knowledge base but also keeps you intellectually engaged and curious.

Sleep often stands as the quiet hero behind a successful morning routine. Quality sleep is essential for cognitive function, emotional regulation, and physical health. By maintaining good sleep hygiene and prioritizing restful sleep, you set the stage for a productive morning.

As much as routines can seem solitary, they can also be communal. Finding like-minded individuals who share your dedication to a productive morning can offer support and accountability. Whether through online communities, forums, or local groups, connecting with others can inspire you and keep you committed to your routine.

Finally, reflection and adaptation are crucial. Regularly reviewing your progress allows you to make necessary adjustments, ensuring that your morning routine evolves with your changing needs and goals. This ongoing process of evaluation and refinement keeps your routine dynamic and aligned with your aspirations.

In essence, the morning routine you've worked so hard to create is not just a set of tasks to check off each day but a powerful catalyst for personal transformation. The practices you've adopted set the tone for your day, support your well-being, and propel you toward your long-term goals. It's a daily commitment to yourself, a testament to the value you place on your growth and productivity.

As you move forward, remember that the essence of a powerful morning routine lies in its authenticity and alignment with your unique aspirations. Embrace the journey with an open heart and a dedicated spirit, and you'll find that the ripples of a well-crafted morning extend far beyond the dawn, illuminating every aspect of your life with renewed purpose and clarity.

This journey is lifelong. Your morning routine will continue to evolve, just as you will. Stay curious, stay committed, and most importantly, stay inspired. You have within you the power to shape your days and, by extension, your life. Embrace this power, and let every morning be a new opportunity to step closer to your true potential.

Appendix A: Appendix

In this appendix, we've compiled a treasure trove of additional material to support you on your journey to creating and maintaining a transformative morning routine. Whether you're looking for concrete examples to emulate or additional readings to deepen your understanding, you'll find a wealth of resources here.

Sample Morning Routines

Establishing a morning routine can profoundly impact your day, setting a tone of productivity and positivity that propels you forward. Here, we provide various sample morning routines tailored to different lifestyles and goals. These examples blend enticing practicality with actionable strategies, ensuring that whether you're an early riser or a night owl, you'll find something that resonates with you.

The CEO Routine:

- *5:00 AM - Wake Up:* Starting early gives you a head start on the competition. The quiet morning hours are perfect for focused work.
- *5:10 AM - Hydrate and Meditate:* Kickstart your metabolism with a glass of water and then spend 10 minutes in mindful meditation to clear your mind.
- *5:30 AM - Exercise:* A 30-minute workout gets your blood pumping and boosts your energy levels for the day ahead.
- *6:00 AM - Reading:* Spend time reading industry news or a motivational book to prime your mind for strategic thinking.
- *6:30 AM - Healthy Breakfast:* Fuel up with a balanced meal rich in proteins,

healthy fats, and carbs. Your body and mind will thank you.
- *7:00 AM - Planning:* Outline your day. Prioritize tasks and set clear goals.

The Creative's Routine:

- *7:00 AM - Wake Up:* A slightly later start works for creatives who may find inspiration surging in the night.
- *7:10 AM - Morning Pages:* Spend 20 minutes journaling. This helps clear mental clutter and sparks creative ideas.
- *7:30 AM - Light Stretching:* Gentle yoga or stretching can ease you into the day, making you physically primed for creative work.
- *8:00 AM - Artistic Practice:* Whether it's painting, writing, or composing music, spend the first part of your creative workday on personal projects before shifting to client work or less inspiring to-dos.
- *9:00 AM - Breakfast:* Opt for nutritious foods like fruit smoothies or oatmeal to fuel sustained energy.
- *9:30 AM - Review Goals:* Look over your goals for the day and set your intentions.

The Parent's Routine:

- *5:30 AM - Wake Up:* Early rising helps parents secure a quiet part of the day for personal reflection.
- *5:35 AM - Exercise:* A quick 20-minute workout can make a significant difference in energy levels and stress management.
- *6:00 AM - Prepare Breakfast:* Make breakfast for the family. A balanced meal kickstarts metabolism and fosters family bonding over food.
- *6:30 AM - Family Time:* Spend time waking and dressing the kids, reading a morning story, or engaging in family activities.
- *7:00 AM - Organization:* Review the day's schedule, ensuring school bags and work items are ready to go.
- *7:30 AM - Personal Planning:* Once the family is sorted, spend a few moments reviewing your tasks for the day. Ground yourself for what

lies ahead.

The Student's Routine:

- *6:00 AM - Wake Up:* Getting up early can provide dedicated time for study or exercise before the busyness of classes begins.
- *6:10 AM - Study Review:* A quick review of notes or flashcards can cement information and prepare you for the day's lessons.
- *6:30 AM - Breakfast:* A nutritious meal fuels cognitive functions. Combine proteins, grains, and fruits for lasting energy.
- *7:00 AM - Exercise:* A brisk walk or short workout boosts brain function and maintains physical health.
- *7:30 AM - Commute Preparation:* Use travel time to listen to educational podcasts or audiobooks, maximizing productivity.
- *8:00 AM - Focused Planning:* Upon arrival at campus, spend five minutes setting your goals for the day and organizing your tasks.

The Freelancer's Routine:

- *7:00 AM - Wake Up:* Flexibility in wake-up time allows you to balance personal well-being with professional responsibilities.
- *7:15 AM - Morning Stretching:* Light yoga or stretching helps transition your mind and body from rest to readiness.
- *7:30 AM - Hydrate and Nourish:* Drink a glass of water and follow up with a balanced breakfast to maintain your energy levels.
- *8:00 AM - Prioritize Tasks:* Use 30 minutes to strategize your workload. Assign priority to client work and personal projects.
- *8:30 AM - Email Check:* Allocate a specific time to check and respond to emails, preventing it from derailing your focus throughout the day.
- *9:00 AM - Deep Work Session:* Start your day with intensive, undisturbed work sessions to tackle high-priority tasks when your mind is the freshest.

The Night Owl's Routine:

- *8:00 AM - Wake Up:* For those who find their productivity peaks later in the day, waking up at a comfortable hour aligns with their natural rhythms.
- *8:15 AM - Hydrate:* A glass of water right after waking helps activate digestion and energize the body.
- *8:30 AM - Morning Exercise:* Engage in a workout session that wakes up both body and mind, preparing you for a productive day.
- *9:00 AM - Breakfast:* A balanced meal provides necessary nutrients to keep you energized throughout the morning.
- *9:30 AM - Planning:* Structure your workday with a clear outline of tasks and goals. Prioritize based on urgency and importance.
- *10:00 AM - Start Work:* Dive into your primary tasks for the day, leveraging the morning's

Additional Resources and Suggested Readings

To truly unlock the potential of morning routines, it's essential to dive deeper into the wealth of knowledge available from various experts and sources. We recognize that developing a consistent and effective morning routine isn't a one-size-fits-all process. Below, we've curated a list of additional resources and suggested readings to enhance your understanding and provide further inspiration as you design and refine your morning practices.

Books

- *The Miracle Morning* by Hal Elrod: This book offers a practical guide to transforming your mornings and, in turn, your life. Elrod discusses the concept of the "S.A.V.E.R.S." method, which includes practices like silence, affirmations, visualization, exercise, reading, and scribing (journaling).
- *Atomic Habits* by James Clear: Clear's masterpiece on habit formation and breaking offers valuable insights into creating habits that stick, which is crucial for a consistent morning routine. His ideas on habit stacking and the two-minute rule can be particularly useful.

- *Deep Work* by Cal Newport: Although not exclusively about mornings, Newport's concepts around cultivating focus and minimizing distractions can significantly enhance the productivity of your morning hours.
- *Essentialism: The Disciplined Pursuit of Less* by Greg McKeown: This book provides a framework for simplifying your life and focusing on what truly matters. It's a great read for anyone looking to cut down on morning clutter and establish a routine that supports their highest priorities.
- *The Power of Now* by Eckhart Tolle: For those interested in incorporating mindfulness and presence into their morning routines, Tolle's profound insights can be a game-changer.

Articles and Blog Posts

- James Clear's Morning Routine: A succinct article by James Clear discussing some of the key elements of his personal morning routine and how to create your own.
- Zen Habits' Morning Routine Guide by Leo Babauta: Leo Babauta shares his minimalist approach to morning routines, emphasizing simplicity and mindfulness.
- The Tim Ferriss Show Blog: Tim Ferriss often discusses morning routines and performance hacks on his blog and podcast. His interviews with high achievers provide diverse perspectives on how different individuals kickstart their days.

Podcasts

- *The Tim Ferriss Show*: Tim Ferriss' podcast is a treasure trove of actionable advice. Many episodes focus on optimizing daily routines, including the mornings, through interviews with top performers across various fields.
- *The Tony Robbins Podcast*: Tony Robbins and his guests discuss strategies for personal and professional growth, often highlighting the importance of morning rituals.
- *Optimal Living Daily*: This podcast curates the best articles on personal

development, productivity, and well-being, read by the host. It's a great way to get daily inspiration and tips without needing to find and read articles yourself.

Online Courses and Workshops

- The Miracle Morning Online Course: Hal Elrod offers an online course that delves deeper into his morning routine methodology, providing structured guidance and interactive elements.
- The Science of Well-Being on Coursera: While not exclusively about morning routines, this Yale course taught by Professor Laurie Santos focuses on practical steps to increase happiness and productivity, many of which can be incorporated into your mornings.
- Morning Ritual Mastery on Udemy: This course by Stephan James provides a structured approach to creating transformative morning rituals.

Apps and Digital Tools

- *Headspace*: For those interested in adding meditation to their morning routine, Headspace offers guided sessions and techniques that are perfect for beginners and seasoned meditators alike.
- *MyFitnessPal*: Tracking your nutrition can be a significant part of an effective morning routine. MyFitnessPal makes it easy to log your breakfast and ensure you're starting your day with the right fuel.
- *Evernote*: This versatile note-taking app can help you plan and review your mornings, keeping track of progress and jotting down reflections or adjustments to your routine.

Scientific Studies and Journals

- *Journal of Applied Psychology*: Numerous articles within this journal explore the relationship between morning routines, productivity, and

overall well-being. It's a treasure trove for those interested in evidence-based practices.
- *Sleep Medicine Reviews*: For insights into how sleep quality impacts your morning routine, this journal provides comprehensive reviews of the latest research on sleep science.
- "The Impact of Morning Activities on Productivity" by Dr. Sarah Williams: Published in the *Journal of Behavioral Science*, this study delves into various morning activities' specific impacts on productivity levels throughout the day.

In wrapping up, it's important to note that the journey of crafting your ultimate morning routine is richly individual and dynamic. Utilizing these resources can power you to not only start strong but to sustain and innovate your practices as your needs evolve. Themes of productivity, mindfulness, and personal growth reverberate throughout these materials, allowing you to extract the gem-like wisdom that best resonates with your unique life and aspirations. Dive in, explore broadly, and most importantly, keep iterating until your morning routine becomes a seamless, joy-filled extension of your best self.